Empty Roads & Broken Bottles
In search for
The Great Perhaps

The Glass Child

Charlotte Eriksson

Discography
Charlotte Eriksson *EP, 2011*
I Will Lead You Home *single, 2011*
This Is How Ghosts Are Made *EP, 2011*
Songs of An Insomniac *EP, 2011*
Letdown *single, 2012*
Who Am I *single, 2012*
Stay *single, 2013*
I'd Like To Remain A Mystery, *album 2013*
I'd Like To Remain A Mystery *Acoustic Edition, 2013*
Love Always, Your Tragedy *EP, 2013*
The Fall *single, 2014*
I Must Be Gone, or Stay and Die, *album 2014*

All my love to
Angela Mastrogiacomo, Keely Knightley and Alice Duff
for proofreading and helping me correct my Swedishness,
and Niels Bakx for playing and recording with me from the start.
All my love to you who ever wrote something to me online, through a letter or
through email. About my writings, my music or just simple little words. Every single
message has a place in this book and every little word helped me create this, inspired
me to not give up. I take pride in being independent, in standing on my own two
feet and even in my solitude, but I would not be where I am today if it wasn't for all
the beautiful people I've been lucky to meet, talk to or get to know on this journey.
Even if it was just a "hi" in school, a smile while running to the bus or a close
friendship that went wrong. If it was ugly words about my music, negative thoughts
about the way I choose to live my life, or even you who never believed I could do
this;
You all shaped me, turned me into who I am today,
forced me to reach higher, work harder, search deeper,
and I wouldn't change a thing.

Contents

7. I am alone in a hostile world.
   14. The Becoming.
   20. I must be gone and live or stay and die.
   21. Facing fear and stepping out of yourself.
   26. Having no destination, I am never lost.
   30. I wheeled with the stars, no witness but the moon.
   33. Though I sang in my chains like the sea.
   36. You're beautiful but you're empty.
   40. It takes courage to grow up and become who you really are.
   42. You will either step forward into growth, or you will step backward into safety.
   51. You know who you are, you just have to believe it.
   52. Once I was beautiful, now I am myself.

57. Journals
   62. Following the heroes.
   69. Learning fire – You love, you burn.
   83. Sep 26, 2012 - Destruction, the art of destroying.
   88. An early morning letter.
   98. On Love.
   100. Duende. The possibility of loss.
   104. They all wanted me to shrink.
   106. I Will Love You Like The World Is Ending.
   108. Someone should have told me this.
   111. I was too hard to love.

114. Epilogue - Amor Fati.

Pack light,
Throw your keys in the river and cancel all your contracts. Grab a guitar, bring your best friends and hit the road. See the world, taste the ocean and feel the concrete under your bare feet. Play music with no witness but the moon, with no concern of who's listening or what they think. Dance in the rain, sleep under the stars and taste as much of the universe as you can. Here's to cheap wine straight from the bottle, coffee in the morning with someone you love and intelligent conversations about things that matter, roses and butterflies. Here's to escapism, and new beginning every day. To libraries, coffee shops and foreign cities where no one knows your name. Here's to facing our fears, to all the things, views and feelings yet to be discovered, yet to be explored.
Here's to all the beautiful things we will see
and grow to be.
Here's to how I found you,
and here's to how you found me.

I am alone in a hostile world.

People only want to know the glory of the man standing on top of the mountain. They want to see the hero, make up the story in their heads and ignore the truth. We all want to believe in the hero. We need to believe that he exists; believe that what we are striving for is possible. That a person can become all these things we wish to become and experience all these things we wish to experience. People need to believe in the hero, but they only want to see some parts of him. They only want to see the glory of him standing on top of the mountain.

People don't want to know that he almost died in the process of climbing the mountain. They don't want to know that he fell several times and that his fingers are frozen. That he's got open wounds and they're infected and aching. That he's standing at the top with tears in his eyes, completely out of breath. They only want to see the glory of him standing there. I know, that's how we work. I want to believe in heroes too, and I do. I believe that there is no limit for how great and beautiful we can be. I believe that there is no limit for how wide and recklessly we can live. How much we can feel, explore, see and be. I believe in the hero too,

but I refuse to believe in your kind.

I don't believe in the hero that sets out to climb a mountain and achieves it with no setbacks. If he does, he obviously didn't set his goals high enough and shouldn't even have anything to be proud of. He didn't challenge himself enough. He might have learned a thing or two, but the real lessons are taught when you're balancing on the very edge, with one foot over the cliff, everyone expecting you to fall. That's when you realise your potential. Or rather, how far away from your own potential you actually are. A hero is not someone who's born with a talent and therefore learns to run faster than every man in the world, or who is born with the biggest vocal range, or who wakes up smiling every day with no dark thoughts. That's effortless, lazy and safe and has nothing to do with heroism. The hero is the one who beats the odds, who chooses to not take the conventional road just because that's where he's expected to be. The hero takes the road no one thought he would, hearing people screaming "no" behind him, but keeps walking anyway because the hero is the one who **does what people thought he could not do**. A hero is someone who **doesn't give up**. Who's falling and losing and crying and doubting but keeps walking anyway, because **he does not give up. He can not give up.**

It's about personal development. It's about creating your own character and pushing it to the limit. It's about pushing yourself so far out of your own and everybody else's idea of who you are and what you're capable of, that you no longer believe in limits. It's about reaching beyond your so-called potential, because your potential is never where you or anyone else expects it to be, not even close. It's about being able to say with the last breath of your life **"I used all my potential and all my talents and pushed myself to the limit. I could not have fought any harder."**

But please remember that my limits, my personal beliefs and my personal philosophy, have nothing to do with yours.

I'm a storyteller; I'm created by made-up worlds in my head, that's how I can create the world I want to live in. That's how I can write my life in the way I wish to remember it, in the way I wish to experience it. But I would never write anything that isn't true.

This journey, is all about me.

I'm sorry.

Our true heroes are the ones that made mistake after mistake, but kept going. The wisest people are the ones that know defeat; who know sorrow, pain and survival. A wise person, a person who I look up to, is someone who is forever exploring and questioning himself; in solitude, in interaction with other people, in the city, in the forest, with no money, with loads of money; who never considers himself wise or talented or educated, because he knows that there is so much more to learn and to be. The hero can't invest too much energy into what other people think of him because he is too busy studying himself. He knows his own mind so well that nothing can take away his character. They know how to control their own destiny, how to take their lives in their own hand, how to not be placed in any situation, but how to choose it. Or, they at least know how to choose their own place in every situation. I believe that life will never throw you anything that you can't handle. I believe that when there's a storm coming in, it's up to you to either curse it and run in to hiding, or to embrace the challenge, be curious about what you can learn, and excited to see who you will be when you come out on the other side.

I could choose to just tell you about all the beautiful things I see. I could choose to only tell you about all the amazing people I get to meet, about the open road, the world and all the adventures that are waiting to be explored out there. I could tell you about the many opportunities, possibilities and beautiful things there are outside these walls, that door and this town. I could write about how I feel when I sing, write and create something from heartbreak, sorrow, sadness or just simply nothingness. How nothingness can become the most beautiful, unexplainable feeling that makes you forget about gravity for an hour. How art makes me forget about all these things that people tell me to become and do, and all these ugly words I've been told. About all these people I've met and loved and lost. I could tell you about how I left everything I knew in Sweden, younger than my age but still with questions and longings worth a life-time, to redesign myself. To revalue myself, or rather, find any kind of value in myself.

How I've spent nights on the concrete unable to find any kind of worthiness in this shell of body; because one's body, I've learned, does not come connected with the mind. Oneness, being connected with your whole being, is something you need to learn. It's a skill, and I am struggling.

How I have lost and loved and won and cried myself to the person I am today. How I changed and rearranged my dreams and goals at least a million times and how I still wake up every morning, asking myself what my dream is today; who I am today, or at least, who I'd like to become today. How I detached myself from society, my family and friends, and embarked on a journey in solitude with a carefully planned distance between my inner thoughts and my actions; my language, the words I spoke and the words I wrote. And how free I am, or at least how free I thought I was until I realised that freedom had nothing to do with being alone, with not owning keys, not having a home or not having friends. Freedom, I learned, is about feeling that you belong in your own body; that your mind, your physicality and your heart are one, connected to whatever nature you have. I thought that if I owned nothing, had nothing, was nothing, I would have nothing left to lose, and I wouldn't be scared anymore. Because my whole life I've been so damn scared. Scared to live because I was scared to die. But at the same I was so scared of living, so I wanted to die. Or maybe so scared of dying that I refused to live. You don't have to be afraid to fall, when you're already on the ground. You don't have to be scared to lose someone, when there's no one around to lose.

I could write about how you're filled with a calmness when you decide that you don't care about survival. The second you realise you're not attached to your own life and not obligated to care for a long future. How freeing it is to know that your only task is to live in the here and now, and to live better and wilder than anyone thought you could. How I laughed at them all, stupid dead-walking people, whom through my eyes were waking up, doing the same tasks without a heart every single day just to afford a future that would look exactly the same until they one day realised that that was their youth, their lives, and they let it pass them by. Empty efforts with empty hearts. Cluttering thoughts spinning around with no answers. And how I wandered around, trying so hard to live, until I one day realised that I too was wasting my youth by not realizing that this journey, the 'becoming', is my life, and there's no finish line. This is it.

I am climbing the mountain, and I'm right in the beginning. There are days when I look down at the people I left behind, still telling me to come back, to surrender to comfort and company. There are days when I feel so weak that I can't take any more steps; when I fall on my aching knees and scream to whatever God there is up there, asking why the hell he can't help me, guide me, tell me where I'm supposed to go. There are nights when I lie awake wondering if this really means anything in the end, if it really makes a difference. Every day I wonder; does it really mean anything at all if there's no one around to share it with? My wish has always been to write my own story, to create a life that's worth writing about. But is a story worth anything at all if I have no one to tell it to?

I started this journey in an attempt to create a life worth writing about, and this is when I make the choice to share it with you. Because a story is born when it's being told. I'm climbing the mountain and this is where I've built my home. This mountain is my life; the top, is the end, and I am here to tell you about my way there. I am here to tell you about all these beautiful things I get to see and these glorious experiences I have. The views, the ocean, the flowers, how the air is changing with every step; about all the people I meet on my way up, the ones that want to give up, the ones that are on their way down, defeated, the ones that stopped half way to enjoy the surroundings and never got going again.

But most of all, I'm here to kill your hero. I'm here to tell you about the real climb, the real mountain; the stepping-stones that break, the beasts that no one warned me about, the storm that killed my fire and stole my friends. I want to tell you about all the friends and dreams and beliefs I've lost on the way, but also about the new beliefs I have. The new dreams I've realised. The new friends I've met. Friends who taught me lessons, showed me how to share and told me stories I never thought I'd hear. How I've experienced energy; how the hands of two people can create a fire so strong that my tired little heart started to race like it has never done before. I want to tell you about leavings and apologies and a missing so strong that you literally want to take a knife and cut your heart out. About how it never gets easier to say goodbye no matter how many times you do it, and how I'd like to spend my life arriving in new cities every morning. How I wish for company and someone to share this with, but at the same time how I crave solitude and places far, far away. I want to tell you about real love, so poetic that I could write thousands of poems and never-ending novels about it. And how it all stops when you lose that love. How the world keeps spinning, the people keep walking and the tube keeps running, but my world stopped. And how I couldn't see how I could possibly exist again, be again. But how you keep on walking anyway, because what else is there to do? How I gave myself away with every word I sang, to every fan I gained, to every critic I met. And finally, how I learned that I needed to belong to myself again. To live with myself again.

I am here to tell you about my journey to the top of the mountain. The real journey. A real story about a girl who set out on a never-ending adventure that became a beautiful fight for self-acceptance, humbleness, personal philosophy, growth, real people, self-discovery, passion, love, loss and what real naked art means.

This is my story. I'm not sure where I want to end up, but I know where I'm going and I'm on my way. It might not always be easy, but it will always be beautiful.

The Becoming

Somewhere in England, June 2012

Dirty windows and doors I can't open. Sleeping on the floor with three layers of hoodies because that's what I'm used to, that's what I know. And because it's summer but I'm cold and never hungry. I'm twenty and I feel small. Getting smaller and getting older. Some days it's okay. It's more than okay, some days I'm even happy. I wake up and I laugh. I sing and tell myself that I'm exactly where I want to be, on my way to who I want to be. Some days. Most of the days I'm cold and small and I'm getting addicted to the dizziness of low blood sugar. Sometimes all I need is your hands and your voice, telling me that it will be okay, it will be okay, it will all be okay. But most of the time I still crave the running away, the escaping like a ghost, never to be seen or heard again.

It was a very ordinary day, the day I packed my life in a bag and bought a one-way train-ticket to nowhere. It's like how you suddenly can see your own breath the first day of winter - everything is insignificant until you start thinking about it, and I'd had enough of my own uselessness. I'd spent two years in London, in a crappy little room where I could fit a small bed that creaked as soon as you moved, my guitar, and I could barely open the door. I'd spent 18 months striving and fighting to simply *become*, ripping every fibre of my being out for the world to take, but it wasn't received very well. Mostly empty words about the standard of my

14

productions, my sound, my so-called image that I needed to 'define'. It's a 24-hour consuming mission that you give your soul to, with nothing in return but a little self-fulfilment now and then when you manage to forget about the world out there for an hour and create melodies and words out of nothingness. That unexplained emotion from creating. Money becomes a rarely seen myth, and so after 18 months I was faced with the choice of either getting a day-job - spend my days doing tasks without a heart just to pay the rent for my crappy room that was covered in written words about leaving and oceans, or to give up my steady base, a home, the paying to the system and simply live... free. All I wanted was to live a life where I could be me, and be okay with that. I had no need for material possessions, money or even close friends with me on my journey. I never understood people very well anyway, and they never seemed to understand me very well either. All I wanted was my art and the chance to 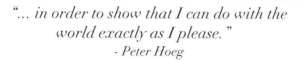 be the creator of my own world, my own reality. I wanted the open road and new beginnings every day.

> "... in order to show that I can do with the world exactly as I please."
> - Peter Hoeg

I had spent my whole life trying to survive, holding on, without even knowing what I was holding on to. I was shaped and born in Sweden, Gothenburg, and there were days when I thought I knew what it felt like to have a home. I was an ordinary kid, living an ordinary life in a very ordinary family. We had a house and two cars and the Swedish distance between feelings and behaviour. I was clever and easily taught, best in my class and good at sports. Never too loud and never too quiet. I was a daughter to be proud of, until I turned ten and realised that this way of living doesn't make sense. I started to question, read about other places, other worlds, how other people lived and I suddenly woke up and couldn't find one single reason to go to school and get through the day. I was an ordinary kid to be proud of until I got to ten and instead turned into a daughter who refused to eat, ran for hours every day and wrote words all over her walls with question marks after them. I grew quiet, distant, guarded. The Swedish unwritten rule about what's accepted to talk about and what's not told me that questions about what it means to love, to be me, why I should eat and why I should sleep, was not okay to speak out loud about. No one could explain to me why being solitary was so wrong, why they all wanted me to interact with other people, why you shouldn't starve to the point of passing out and what was so terribly wrong with spiking your coffee at 10am in school. You were called spoiled, ungrateful and 'a teenager', and so I turned inwards instead. I grew solitary trying to observe how other people lived with themselves, trying to figure this whole thing out on my own. I grew a consuming hatred towards my own self, my own body, my own mind. I couldn't accept my limitations and weaknesses and I just simply couldn't find a way to live with myself. I've spent years studying my own mind and sadness, but I still haven't figured out how someone can grow to hate her own self so much. To the degree of breaking mirrors while catching her own reflection for a short second. (It took me months to learn how to live with a mirror in my room in London without breaking it.)

I spent my youth like this, observing other people. Trying to learn how to live and trying to figure out how to be someone. But I never really found a way to fit in or stand out and I lost myself in the crowd and people's expectations. They expected me to have answers and be interested in things I couldn't care less about. They stumbled on, doing tasks without a heart, ignoring my questions about why – why?! I tried to find answers from old writers, authors and artists, and art simply became my escape. It gave me heaven for an hour because when I got lost in the story, in the music, in my own writing, it finally wasn't about me and my reality anymore. I found an escape from that town and my own personality. Through music and writing I could create a new world, a new self where things made more sense. Where sad and broken things could be considered beautiful and where all these material dreams were of no value. So I searched for the definition of being me in poetry, music and literature, but even though it became my safe place it all just opened my eyes even more. Widened my world even more, triggering my confusion even more. And so as soon as I was done with my last years of struggling in school (which was a matter of finding reasons to just simply show up every day) I bought a one-way plane ticket to London, hoping to never come back again.

I must be gone and live,
or stay and die
- Shakespeare

The beginning in London was a long, long year of learning and becoming. Of revaluing and redesigning myself and my priorities. Not only by learning the hard way about playing music, but personally, as the person I'd grown to be. Or rather to become the person I wanted to be. I wanted to leave the old me, my old habits, my old scars behind, but living in solitude only fed the monsters. I didn't know anyone or anything, and so being forced to live in my mind 24/7 with no one and nothing to distract me from myself, I had no choice but to face my demons. I found myself locked in the crappy little room I was renting in North West London, dealing with everything I'd done, every version I had been, every person I had met. It was either to deal with the past and accept it, or to be held back by it.

What I realised was that I can't run from anything I've done or who I've been, but I can learn to use it. I can learn to grow from it, treat it as stepping-stones, experiences. Turn it into stories, melodies, poetry and art. Make the choice to remember my life as the poem I want to be remembered as, as the story I'd like to leave behind. I don't want to look back on my first twenty years and remember it as a dark long struggle to be. I want to remember how I grew my strength and searched in the deepest corners of myself. How much I saw, felt and learned.

While digging up old skeletons, my story slowly started to take shape. In an attempt to figure out how to live and what this was all meant to be about I found myself consumed in other people's stories. I was hypnotized by how these writers, philosophers and musicians had lead lives that were worth writing about, reading about, and how other people could learn about themselves by just knowing how these long lost thinkers lived. I realised that they all had been struggling with the simple pleasure of being alive, but they had all used it to create something that wouldn't be able to exist if it wasn't for their struggle. They had all used their pain to write their stories. To create their art. And that became my hope.

So there I was, 18 years old with nothing but my own past, a dream and a future to create in any way I wanted to. No commitments and no one to please. Just a blank page to fill with whatever I wanted my world to be filled with. Whatever I wanted the world to receive from me.

I figured, if these old writers can make me feel less alone by telling me about their lives, then maybe there is someone else out there who might feel what I feel. Who is struggling like I do and who can tell me that I'm not alone. I thought to myself, that maybe if I learn to sing loud and strong enough, if I become so good that they just can't deny me, then maybe I will be heard and someone can confirm my belief that there are more people who feel what I feel. And maybe I can create my life in a way that makes me want to hold on to it. Maybe I can learn to live in a way that makes it worth writing about, and maybe I can actually become something more than this empty shell. And all these people back home, who laughed at me, waiting for my failure? I thought to myself, that maybe if I fought hard enough I could show them all that they didn't break me. That I didn't fade away like they all thought I would. That I survived. That I used all these things to build my strength, and that I found a way.

So I practiced, every single day. I found a way to use my

disciplined athlete-mind to get up at 6am every morning and not waste one single second, a second that I could use to develop and become better. I learned everything I could find about vocal technique, singing, writing and song-writing. And just as my old figure-skating coach taught me – if you want something bad enough, you can always find a way to get it. So the results came, and I could slowly start to use my voice in a way that expressed what I felt and what I wanted them to hear. I never wanted to be a professionally trained singer, I've never even cared about range or how many scales I can do. All I ever wanted to do as a singer was to be able to express myself in the way that I needed to. To be able to use my voice in the way that I hear these words, melodies and voices in my head. I want people to hear my mind, hear my heart, hear my soul. Not a perfectly trained vocal technique. (Which I will never have anyway, I just wasn't born a singer.)

After a couple of months like this, I had grown more than I had done during my 18 years in Sweden. I couldn't remember who I was before I moved and I felt hardened. Not necessarily stronger, but not so unsure. Clearer, not so detached. More focused, not so blurry. After months in solitude I wanted to test my character. So I forced myself to step out of my comfort zone and go out and connect with people. I realised that no one knew me here. I could become whoever I wanted to be for these people, and that became my courage.

Facing fear and stepping out of yourself.

To this day, I don't consider myself a singer or a performer. I don't have it in my blood. Some girls are just born to be performers in all kinds of ways. They're entertainers. I remember girls in school when I was younger, always so damn sure about themselves and their place. They sing and dance, act and talk without thinking and just love being in the spotlight, on the stage, in front of people. I didn't. I hated it with all my heart. I was the girl who turned red when I was asked a question in class, even though I always knew the answer. I was the girl who skipped the classes when we had presentations in order to save myself from the 'naked in front of your whole school'-dream. And I was the girl who locked myself in the toilet during lunchbreak in order to not have to eat. I was never bullied, I was not really a loner, and I wasn't considered an outsider. I just never understood the other kids and the things that amused them never seemed to make sense to me. What they talked about didn't interest me, and when I tried to talk about things that I cared about they didn't even understand. I just didn't get it, them, or how they wasted time playing meaningless games. How they dressed or how they asked stupid questions about the simplest tasks in class. And so I just wanted to be left alone, and I even think the other kids respected me for that. They let me be, respectfully. This, of course, left me very independent from my early childhood, which is a good skill, but it also meant that I never learned how to interact with other people in a comfortable way. I never learned what it means to be a friend or what it's like to have someone close. I never learned to trust or to let people in, and I never learned to depend on others. I grew guarded to both kids in my age and my family, and I was always watching my back. I always had a weird feeling of being in everyone's way, as if they were out to get me. I felt haunted. I've always felt so damn haunted. It's not that hard to figure out that living with a feeling of being haunted, and making the choice to pursue music and therefore standing on stage, just doesn't really match.

When I first started to play live-shows I was nervous to the point of nausea. I had never played a real gig before I moved to London and that was one of the reasons to why I chose London – it's the capital of live-music and open mic nights. I was still in the process of re-creating myself when I made the decision to expand my identity and push myself out of my head. To face my fears and do something I was scared of. The difference though, was that the more I thought about it, the more I found comfort in the fact that playing my music at a stage would be nothing more than a couple of minutes of acting. And acting was something I was a master at by now. I found comfort in the fact that no one knew me in London, no one knew where I was from or who I'd been and I could basically make myself out to be whoever I wanted to be that night.

This is a thing I do, even today, and I know that putting on masks and faking your identity is wrong, but I dare to say that if it wasn't for this little ritual, I would still live in Sweden, scared to face the world and my dreams.

I found some different open mics, took my guitar, left my insecurities in my flat and put on a mask. I faked my confidence, put on a smile and went up and sang my heart out. I forced my faked identity to start conversations with the other musicians, with the bar-people, the sound-guys and the people that I noticed were listening when I played. And I did it with a smile, without flickering my eyes – but with a nausea so huge that I went to throw up behind the venue right after I left.

It's a funny thing, overcoming your fears. You feel sick while you're doing it, like you have a thousand knives in your chest telling your nature that what you're doing is wrong, not what you're supposed to do. But when it's over, every night on the tube home, I felt like I was flying. It felt like I was on speed, natural ecstasy, high on adrenaline. I could do anything! And that's the point. Doing something you thought you couldn't do is the most amazing feeling in the whole world. That's what it should be all about – beating the odds, proving yourself wrong. And it's addictive. You're going to want to do it again. You want to feel that adrenaline-kick, fly higher and push yourself further, and that's how you grow and expand your character.

After a few times I wasn't even nervous when I went up on the stage and I could easily start a conversation with anyone without the stabbing knives in my chest. I stumbled upon conversations with musicians and producers who wanted to collaborate, promoters who wanted to book me, managers who wanted to be involved and I slowly built myself a little network of contacts, and it wasn't as scary anymore.

Another point I'd like to make is that I never really cared about all those contacts. I wasn't interested in these managers or producers. I never wanted to collaborate or convince another label to like me. I was after the knowledge. This is another chapter, but I simply figured, if I could learn what they know about the industry and the business-side, I can do it all myself, on my own, in my own way.

But most of all, I was after the adrenaline, the kick of doing something I thought I couldn't do. I wanted to burn, set fire to my lungs. This is when you have to raise the bar, push yourself further and harder and find new ways to get that adrenaline, because you won't feel the same rush after doing something a couple of times. Your brain gets used to it, and so you need to jump from an even higher cliff. And this is all how the growing happens, the *becoming*. I'm not suggesting that you should go around and push yourself to be scared every day, but think about it for a second: if you're not constantly scared, you're probably keeping yourself in your comfort-zone. You're not growing, not expanding your identity and you won't become as much and as great as you could be.

This is still how I do things. There was a time when I, for a short while, had this idea of taking a day-job at a clothing store, just to take my mind off the music for a couple of hours every week. I was asked to come in for an interview to a clothing store, and I was terrified. Suddenly I was pushed into a situation that was completely foreign to me. I'd never had a day-job, I didn't know what they wanted me to answer, and I didn't know anything about their world. They asked me about the newest trends, what's in and out, why I would be good for their position and what previous skills I had that made me suitable for the job. And there I sat, completely quiet the first minute, thinking about all the stories I could tell them about living on the road, the people I've met and what the homeless man taught me about love. But that wasn't their world, and their world wasn't a part of mine. I couldn't care less about the newest trends or what was in and out. So I took a deep breath, put on my mask, faked my confidence and my identity, kept my eyes on the interviewer and did what I do best – acted and told a story. I put on the character of a happy and outgoing girl who wanted to have a future in the fashion-industry. I had no idea about the latest trends, but I knew how to act and how to talk in a way that made people believe me. I faked and lied for 30 minutes, hugged the girl who after a while became really friendly, and right after I went to throw up behind the building.

It's not a beautiful skill, to be able to fake and act your way through conversations, but that's how I grow. If it wouldn't be for this way of doing it, I would still be sitting alone in my room, scared to talk to people, scared to say something stupid, or act weird or be misunderstood.

The day after the interview they called and said that I got the job, but of course I said no. Just like talking to all these people at the venues where I played, I wasn't really interested in getting that job. What I wanted was to test myself. To know that I could push myself into a new world, a new business and that my identity and character wasn't limited to my little world that I'd built for myself, within the arts. I believe in knowing who you are but without limiting yourself to your own expectation of who you are.

Let's repeat that:

I believe in knowing who you are but without limiting yourself to your own expectation of who you are.

Because if you do, you're just like all those other people telling you that you're not good enough or that you can't become who you want to become. Every single day you can become something more, something new, something different, if you're open to it.

Having no destination,
I am never lost.
-Ikkyu

I spent 18 years in Sweden trying to become and then fought to build a life in London for almost two years, and there were days when I actually called it my home. There were days when it felt like I was on the right track, on my way to figuring things out. I had my art, my music, my writings. I understood my mind a bit better and I didn't feel as haunted. I was starting to get along with my reflection and I didn't have to break mirrors anymore. Not as often anyway. But then there are a thousand different opinions about your art and your abilities. There's a certain missing and homesickness that comes with leaving your home. There's the solitude, the loneliness, and then there's the money – the rarely seen myth and the choice of either getting a day-job, doing tasks without a heart – or to give up the idea of having a home. My definition of a home was blurred out by a homesickness for somewhere else far, far away anyway, and so I thought: if I give up the idea of having a home, if I make the road and the journey my life, I never have to feel lost because I have no home and no destination and I will be happy wandering forever and ever and ever and. . .

I didn't do music to live; I lived so that I could do music. For so long when I was younger, I woke up and got through one more day just to experience that beauty of music one more time. So to take a day-job, to spend half my day doing something that didn't touch me just to afford a roof over my head, wouldn't be reason enough for me to get up in the morning. I knew it. It would last for a week, maximum, then I would stay longer and longer in bed in the morning, staring at the ceiling, trying to find reasons to get up and get through the day. Until I stopped showing up at that meaningless job anyway. No, I just couldn't do it. And so I figured, the only way out of this system that these people are building for me, is to detach myself completely. To be so free that I have nothing to do with them. I wanted to get out.

So I wrote my last letters of goodbyes and took a random train from Waterloo to nowhere, fighting with every fibre of my being to not feel sad, or lost, or scared. With no witness but the moon, no family but the road, I was hoping to find something that would lead me somewhere.

I can't remember how long I was on the train but it was long enough for empty bottles and cravings for something stronger. I arrived in the morning before the world was awake and existing, and I loved it. There's something about arriving in new cities, wandering empty streets with no destination. I will never lose the love for the arriving, but I'm born to leave.

I spent some days just walking. Walking and drinking and writing. I left my hotel-room filled with empty bottles and instant coffee and came back at night to a sterile and cleaned office, triggering my destruction. I enjoyed it. Setting fire to my lungs. I want to burn with excitement or anger and bleed, bleed out my words. I want to get all fucked up and write raw and ugly about all these things I see and am and could be. But then the echoing words from all the people back home; *"no Charlotte, stay in line, behave. Get good grades, a well-paid job, don't mess up. One chance, no mistakes."*

I spent my whole life striving and fighting to *become*. To become what other people wanted me to be. To become what other people thought I would be. But I wanted so much more, knew I could do so much more. Like this greatness I knew I was capable of, I just needed to find a way to release it, to get out of these walls that I built for myself. I knew I could shake up the scene, make a difference, take people's breath away. I just had to *become*.

I studied myself and wrote my life down. Put it out for the world to take and tear apart. I released 3 EPs and opened myself up in interviews and on social media. I played all over the UK, had one single reaching #2 on the Swedish iTunes chart, got picked up by two managers in New York who flew me over to play some shows, and I gained a beautiful following and started to build an amazingly dedicated fan-base of people who understood what I was singing about. We became a community and I saw how they supported each other daily through Twitter, Tumblr and Facebook and I talked to them every single day. But the 'industry' never got it.

I've spent hours and days travelling to different "well-respected industry people" that you "should" be involved with because "he can get you somewhere". I've had bold guys in costume telling me that they can learn to like me, there's a potential, *if* I colour my hair, change my style, my sound, sing other people's songs, lose weight, take on a more sexy approach or simply try to be anything but me. I've had people telling me that I'm just simply not good enough, I don't have it, and that I should find something else to do.

And so you live like this, day after day, striving and fighting to simply *become*, or even better – to be. Something better, something more. Something you can live as, live with. A little more developed, a little more defined and de-cluttered. But then there's the people, the world, telling you over and over again who you are and what you actually like and who you actually want to be, and so that real voice in your head speaks softer every day, until you one day wake up and it's gone. They killed it, these bastards, with their empty words and useless talks. These people who are acting like stones, walking without bending their knees, without rolling their feet. Talking with empty words and doing tasks without a heart. They broke it. Drowned it. These damned "experts".

So I packed light and spent months on the road, homeless but at home. Lost yet unable to be lost because I had no destination. I arrived in new cities every morning, scraped coins to afford coffee and then tried to find the busiest venue in town where I begged them to let me play a set or two. If I was lucky I sold enough albums to afford the train the next day. If I was luckier I could afford whiskey and if I was a god damn star I got some tip from the sound-guy. You read and write and sing and experience, thinking that one day these things will build the character you admire to live as. You love and lose and bleed best you can, to the extreme, hoping that one day the world will read you like the poem you want to be. One day, things will change and you will not have to struggle every day to convince people that you and your art are good enough. One day, you will be able to be you, and be okay with that.

All I wanted was to be me, and to be okay with that.

I wheeled with the stars
No witness but the moon
- Pablo Neruda

I'm know I'm only 21 and what do I know about life and love and what really matters? But my promise to myself while writing this book was to tell my story, no one else's. To write the story of my life so that I can remember it in the way I want to remember it. To write this down in an attempt to make it matter, to make my story come alive.

I've been to places so beautiful you wouldn't believe. Villages with such beautiful, friendly people, whom offered me a place to sleep for some nights and gave me food and laughter and welcomed me like a long-lost friend. I've been to bigger cities where people couldn't care less if there's a lost girl sleeping on the concrete. I've seen things that made me want to give everything up and live in a trailer in the forest and I've met people who showed me beauty and love and taught me lessons I'm still trying to live by. I've talked to homeless people, telling me about real life, real love and real pain. I've seen how the sun goes up and how the moon appears. I've spent nights on the bare concrete in a foreign town, nights by the ocean under the stars with my guitar and a bottle of whiskey bought with the tip from the sound-guy. I know the difference between a well-built wall and a broken conversation on the other side of it. I've taken random trains to nowhere, with no destination in mind and no money in my pockets, hoping to end up somewhere where I might find something that could give me a sign of where to go. I've woken up at hospitals after passing out from hunger and lack of sleep. I know what it's like to be followed by drunken old men all the way to the police station. I've stumbled into bars and pubs, begging to play a short set, hoping to get to sell some albums to afford a coffee. Or at least hoping to win a new fan or two. But mostly, just because my music became my home. My art, my words, my voice, my story – became my home, my safety, my comfort. It became everything I knew, everything I had left, and that was the only thing I lived for. As long as I had my art, the ability to turn my existence into stories, melodies and poetry, I was content.

It's a strange thing, every time I talk about this with other people. The first thing they mention is the fact that I was alone. "What did your friends say, your family, weren't you lonely?" First of all, loneliness is not to be connected with solitude. Living in solitude for a while is the most important part of finding yourself, at least for me. You cannot expect to get to know yourself if you spend your life being distracted by other people's opinions and views. You need to find your inner voice, the person you really are independent from other people, when no one else is around. Learn the sound of your own pulse when you lay down to sleep. Learn your body, know how long you can walk without food, how hard you can push yourself, how long you can run. Then learn to beat it. Learn to prove to yourself that you're capable of more than your mind and body tells you to. And then, when you know yourself to the very core, you can expand your identity from other people's minds. Living in solitude is the most beautiful thing. The most scary, yes. But damn, you learn.

There's no way I can tell you about that year on the road and do it justice. It's too huge. The place this experience has in me is bigger than words can tell. It has shaped me in every single way. I just wish there was a way to explain to you how many breath-taking things, people, places, moments and experiences there are out there, and you're blind if you don't let yourself see it. Don't settle for a life within the walls of the system, doing tasks without a heart just because everyone else is living like that. Don't ever stop questioning why you're doing things, why you're living the way you're living. Life is happening out there, outside your window, and I swear, in the end you won't remember the nights you got plenty of sleep and had a healthy breakfast. No, what you will write about in thirty years is the night when you drove on empty streets with the wind in your hair, with a stranger you just met, being stopped by the police and then spent the whole morning laughing about how you talked your way out of it. You won't remember the week when you worked your ass off in the office and then bought an extra expensive dinner. You will remember how you snuck on to the last train to France and wrote stories for 3 hours, hidden in the toilet. And how you learned to say 'thank you' and 'hi' from the French pub-owner, and how he offered you a place to crash in the pub if you played a few songs for some nights. You won't remember how your teacher taught you a new mathematical form. You will remember how you gave a coffee to the homeless man by the river, asked if you could sit down for a while, and how he taught you about the beauty in a simple conversation. I loved living like this, the world before me and new beginnings every day.

I sang in my chains like the sea.
- Dylan Thomas

I built my life like this, the open road and new beginnings every day. In solitude with nothing but me, my mind and my guitar, thinking that if I never get too close to people, if I never let them in, I won't be attached and I won't miss and they won't miss and I can be free - free (what the hell is freedom anyway? Because I had nothing left to lose - no commitments, no keys, no plans, no bills and I never felt so stuck.) I figured I could spend my life like that, running and escaping until I'd had enough. I could pass through life like a ghost, and leave the only thing I could ever love behind – my art. My words, my music, my screwed up little mind. Yes, that's how I wanted to live my life, and when I'd had enough and decided to disappear, they would understand who I really was and I would be remembered as the poem I always wanted to be read as. I'll be the story I tried to live, the myth no one believed in.

But then the seasons change and because of some carefully and randomly chosen words, written together to shape the most beautiful melody they call poetry, I found myself stuck on a journey that slowly killed my fire, both mentally and physically, and I just couldn't stop. I disappeared a little bit every day, but I couldn't get off that Goddamn carousel, that prison I was building for myself. I was so damn free, but I was in chains and in my own prison. Nothing to lose but nothing to gain. You wander foreign streets until you realise that it's not summer anymore, and you increase the layers of clothes while your skin gets paler and you're never really hungry, never really tired but never really rested. Somewhere your becoming has grown into a matter of surviving, of just sticking around. Of hanging on. The process of becoming something better turned out to be your life, and it's happening here and now, passing you by.

I could write a thousand pages about the passage of time and freedom, but I'd also like to tell you about what it's like to be twenty years old and constantly wonder if anyone would notice if you never came back. What it's like to be twenty years old and wonder who's considering themselves close enough to come to your funeral. It's a weird thing, I had this beautiful and exploding following online, people telling me how my music helped them every single day. And I had so many amazing people and friends in my life, but I was like a ghost. I showed up everywhere, laughing, being 'Charlotte', crashed on the couch, just to grab my bag and disappear again the next morning before anyone woke up. I guess I thought that if I never let people get too close, if I never let anyone get to know me enough, I wouldn't be attached, and they wouldn't be attached, and I could keep on leaving, keep running, keep arriving in new cities every day. If you don't get to know anyone well enough, you won't miss them, and missing, I know by now, is one of the most ugly and horrible feelings to live with. Missing, can be like a thousand sharp knives in your chest. They don't kill you, but you're bleeding and it hurts like hell, and so you just have to learn to live with the pain. I learned that you never know how much you need someone, until you don't have them anymore. I, who thought I was completely detached and independent, learned that missing would be my biggest enemy. My greatest downfall.

The most important thing I learned is that living alone has nothing to do with freedom. Owning nothing has nothing to do with freedom. I fought so hard to detach myself from everything, fighting with everything I had to be free, to feel free, but what I really did was build chains for myself. Don't get me wrong, I loved living on the road. I loved the possibilities of what every day could bring. Writing new stories and songs about what I saw every single day. But there's the worrying. There's the constant hunger pains. The fever from the cold and the ache in your muscles. Being unable to really sleep because you still can't relax. The feeling of never feeling at home, and so you think that if you keep leaving, you won't have to worry about not feeling at home, about not belonging, because the world can be your home.

But you can only do this for so long. You can only push your body and your mind to a certain point, until the simple fact that you're human starts to show. I became a prisoner in my own longing for freedom and after a while I just wanted to be lead home.

> You're beautiful but you're empty.
> No one could die for you.
> *- Antoine de Saint-Exupéry, The Little Prince*

One of the biggest challenges I've been forced to face was when, after what felt like a life-time of doing this, going from town to town crashing on people's floors, I started to doubt. I was worn out, tired, uninspired and lonely. When I started this, the pursuing of music, I knew that I would never do it half-heartedly just because I enjoyed it. That's never been who I am and that will never be who I am. If I do something, I go for it with all I am, with all I've got. If I choose to pursue something, I want to become as good as I possibly can be with the potential I've been given, or I won't do it at all. I want the world or nothing. So when I started this I knew that I would give my life to it. And I did, and I don't regret one single second, because if I hadn't put in 24 hours of every day, of being consumed by it for all these years, I would never have been able to get to where I am. I wouldn't have learned in the same way as I did, and most of all I wouldn't have been able to build the fan-base I did, which made it possible for me to actually pursue this full-time. But you can only push yourself for so long. I was 18 years old when I gave up everything else for this, the age when you're supposed to expand your identity and taste as much of the universe as you can, but I spent that time fighting to simply survive.

Somewhere along the way I started to feel drained. There I was with no belongings but my guitar and a few pairs of clothes, ripping my heart out in every single way, but no one seemed to understand what I was saying, what I was singing about, what I tried to do. I screamed my heart out every night, and no one seemed to care. It felt like I pushed and cried and fought and struggled my way through the days, with nothing in return but the so called blessing of getting to do it again the next day. My old friends had stable lives by now with a good education, their own flat, relationships and some of them even well-paid jobs. I had a life built on the only thing I loved, but also a constant fever from sleeping on floors, instant coffee, worn out clothes and some extra pocket money now and then. I loved the idea of living like a wanderer, not owning keys, but if you only knew how tiring constant worrying can be. Exhausting. I was exhausted. Drenched to my bones. You're never really relaxed, always watching your back, always worrying about where to sleep or if you'll afford food the next day. You worry about the future, if things ever will change and if you will find a way one day, and the only reason why you bare to live like this is because of these few minutes on stage every night, when you actually get to do what you love. You do it for the ones that tell you beautiful little words after the show, and most of all, what kept me going every single day for so long, was all these breathtakingly beautiful people whom have been supporting me daily through Twitter, Facebook, Tumblr and Youtube since the start. To go online after a long and struggle-some day and find messages that tell you that your music is helping someone, saving someone, touching someone. That's reason enough to keep going for years, no matter how hard it is.

I wish I could describe the feeling I get when someone says that my music means something to them. It's like 10,000 explosions in your chest that starts a fire and a warmth that refuels every single drenched vein in your body, and you can live on that for days. It's like a sudden burst of clarity of who you are, what you're supposed to do and why you're doing this. It's like a sign of your purpose for being here, your call, your fate. "Of course, how could I ever doubt this" you think to yourself, and suddenly you have every single reason you need in the world to keep going. I never ever thought that I would find people that can take in my lyrics in the same way that I take in my favourite band's lyrics. People send me pictures of my lyrics tattooed permanently on their bodies, of artworks, covers and letters, and I will never learn how to act or what to say in response. I wish there was a word I could use more than 'thank you', so I could explain to them how much they give me, but there are no words for it.

I lived on these feelings, the adrenaline I got from my supporters, for so long, and it pushed me to keep going. But it also became some sort of pressure. Expectations. Suddenly people counted on me. I couldn't let them down. And so I just simply had to keep going, this was the only road I had now. I grew older faster than I thought and as I matured I realised my nature more and more, learned about how other people lived, and I couldn't get rid of that feeling of being lost. I was lost and I didn't know where I was going. I used to have a fire. I used to be unstoppable just because I knew what I wanted and I knew how to get there, and I loved the battle. I used to love proving people and myself wrong. If someone told me that I couldn't do something, I ran uphill with a smile on my face and I lived for the moments when they said "you proved me wrong". But as I had some achievements – I reached #2 on the Swedish iTunes-chart, reached thousands of followers on Twitter and my online sites, got features and interviews requested on a weekly basis, got some sponsors and sold quite a lot of albums both online and at my shows - I realised that I can easily make a living and a life like this. I can do this forever, but is this really how I want to spend my life? Am I happy? Do I even know what happiness is, or what it's supposed to feel like? Do I really use all of my potential this way, or can I be more than this? Is this everything I will ever be, and does this all even matter in the end? Is my music even reflecting this new heart and mind I've grown, or is it just what that insecure and confused girl left behind?

I kept walking that some old road, playing small gigs trying to win over people in the pub one by one, selling a few albums and gaining a few followers online every week. I kept writing new songs every single day, songs that people will probably never hear. I crashed on different floors every night, wherever I could rest my tired little head for some hours. It became a spinning carousel and I couldn't get off, because I didn't know where to go or what to do instead, and I simply didn't have the courage to admit my lack of strength to my followers. I had no real close friends, no real connection with my family, no education, no steady income, no home, and I was lonely. I felt so god damn lonely.

> It takes courage to grow up and
> become who you really are.
> - E.E. Cummings

I needed to take that next step, that next achievement, but I found myself completely numb and empty. I tried to write new goals, new plans, define my dream, but I couldn't find one single goal, couldn't find one single dream that sparked my fire. I remember one day, when I'd had enough of the half-going, the doubting. I wrote myself a bunch of questions to sort my own head out;

Why do you do this? What do you want to get out of it? What's your highest and wildest dream? Who do you want to be in 10 years?

I couldn't find the answer to one single question. I didn't know what I wanted anymore, and if you don't know what you want you will never get anywhere. If there's anything I've learned, it's that there's no reason whatsoever to do something if you don't know why you're doing it and what you want to get out of it. I went back to reading old literature, poetry, got into Zen, studied the teachings of Buddha and Hinduism and practiced meditation. I tried to find answers, definitions, clarity, but I couldn't make sense of my own self, my own journey, my purpose. And so slowly I started to rearrange, re-evaluate and rethink. I slowly started to admit to myself that the music that used to touch me and make me hypnotized didn't even move me anymore. The poetry, the melodies, the feelings that used to leave me breathless just seemed empty and useless. My mind started to wander into other worlds, and I found myself unable to focus. When I was practicing, my mind wandered off and when I tried to sit in front of my computer to do online-marketing I found myself writing long stories and thoughts about philosophies and what it means to live and love. Instead of reading about how to get the perfect snare sound I found myself reading about history, spirituality, philosophy, love, the world and religion. How did other people live and what was their purpose for getting up every morning? I slowly started to admit to myself that I had no fire left. It felt like I'd given all I had, I had nothing left to give, and obviously people didn't understand my art anyway. I found myself numb. I knew I loved music, but I couldn't find that place, that magical place, where nothing else mattered anymore, and so I slowly started to let go, quite unconsciously in the beginning. I stayed in bed, staring at the ceiling for two hours instead of getting up to do my vocal practice. I stopped reading all those marketing and business books. I avoided my email and took weeks to answer the interviews I'd been given. I didn't bother to carry my iPod with me and I couldn't stand hearing music anyway. I couldn't find the energy to keep booking these shows anymore, because it just seemed quite meaningless since they didn't fulfil me, even if I won a few fans every night. I stayed at my friends' houses and took time to actually hang out with them instead of just passing by like a ghost. I actually tried to get to know them and even opened up a little bit about my loss of strength and motivation, and I slowly learned how to build a vague little identity outside of music. For the first time since I started, I let myself go days without practicing or doing online-work, and I experienced new sides of myself. I read a lot, I wrote a lot, I had beautiful conversations with new and old friends until the early mornings and I stayed up night after night trying to cling to this newfound life-style. In a way I was still waiting for my fire to come back so that everything could go back to normal and I could keep pushing, but at the same time I knew that this was bigger.

This was a turning point, a crossroad, and things would change from now on. And all I could do was to either ignore it and keep running blindly on that never-ending road, or I could embrace this change and see where it could lead me. I could follow my heart and simply trust my story.

> You will either step forward into growth,
> or you will step backward into safety.
> - Abraham Maslov

Being flexible

What you'll learn as any kind of freelancer, self-employed or independent person is to be flexible. You learn how to rearrange your goals, plans, time-schedule and days because things change, you change and you cannot possibly know exactly where you want to end up when you start a journey. The most naïve people I know these days are the ones that are so damn sure about every single thing. Who don't question themselves, their choices and their place. I used to be like that, I was 100% sure about what I wanted with my music and my life, and I'm so glad I'm not anymore, because it's limiting. I've been thinking, writing and reading about this a lot because this is something I've been struggling with. I'm reading self-development books from high achievers telling me to write goals and goals and goals and then just fight for your life to get there, spend every second to get closer. But then I'm practicing the teachings of Buddha, Zen, meditation and it's telling me to be in the now, in the present, to forget about the past and the future because it is outside of me, not within my control. This is where you need to create your personal philosophy, finding your own way to live your life, but I think I'm coming to the conclusion that I believe in recreating myself. I believe in long-term goals, yes, but it's about the journey there, every second, every step. The finish line doesn't really matter because you will cross it in less than a second, but the journey will take years.

Every single day I try to wake up and ask myself who I am today, where my heart is and who I want to be when I go to bed tonight. It's about rediscovering yourself every single day, because you should change every single day. If you woke up as the same person as you go to sleep as, you obviously haven't used the day for something worth remembering, right? Every day should have its own poem, its own story, and therefore I've buried my ten-year goals and long-term dreams for a while. I'm focusing on the day-to-day goals. Who can I become today? It might be something just involving my personal philosophy, but I'm learning that it's about seeing the opportunities that today brings. Not what the next ten years can give you. I have a lot left to learn but I think we can learn a lot from the teachings of non-attachment. To learn what we as individuals can cling to and control, and what we can't control. Being in love is something you can't control, you can't cling to it, because the other person's feelings towards you are completely out of your hands and can change at any moment. It's the same with life, the future and what we will become. I've spent my whole life being so damn scared of the future, of what will happen and where I will end up, but if you wake up with the thought that your only task is to live and love but not to cling to it, to let it go when it wants to move on, you stop worrying. You take things as it comes, because it's nature, your story. It's about learning to trust your story.

Being flexible is a skill you need to learn even when it comes to the technical aspect of being a musician. You'll notice that the majority of your career will be affected by people and things outside your power – if you're not very careful with whom you let in. (There's a reason as to why I'm still sitting here without a manager, without a label, without anyone, but that's a different story.) That release-date you set for your album will be ruined because iTunes and Spotify took a month instead of a week to put it up, the recording of your new album is being postponed because your management has another act that they want to focus on instead, that two months long tour you had scheduled and had promoted for months is suddenly cancelled the day before the first show because there's no budget and you just have to suck it up and come up with a new plan. Dealing with setbacks that you can't control is something you will need to learn, I've realised, no matter what you're pursuing in life. If you're an artist, a student or even when it comes to relationships and love. When my plans get crashed my natural instinct is to immediately start working on a new plan of where to go from here in my head. I guess that's what you learn by living day by day on the road, but it's a necessary skill to have in order to never get stuck in a period of wasting time. It's so easy to lose your fire when things don't go your way. When you've been fighting for something with all you've got for so long, and in a second it's taken away from you, or it just fails. I've had setback after setback, rejections and hurdles, and trust me; there were days when I had decided to quit this thing. I've bought more tickets back home than you can imagine and I've been ready to admit my failure. But there is something in me that keeps whispering "just one more day, let's see what can happen," that makes me go on. It's something about the fact that those who never give up, never fail, because they're still going. Something about the fact that if you quit, you will never know what could have happened tomorrow, or just on the other side of that storm. When you're faced with a setback you have two options; either to let it steal your power, or to embrace the challenge and see how much you can learn and grow and use it for your story. The story you're writing, because once again; that is what this is all about. It's about the story you're writing, which is in fact your life, and it's the setbacks, the storms, the dragons and beasts that make a good story.

Now, months later, I can actually sit here and say that the loss of my fire, my doubting, was the best thing that could have happened to my artistic career. Or actually the best thing that could have happened to me in every single aspect of my life. When I found myself in that low I couldn't see the light, I was stuck, depressed and tired. But now from a perspective I can see all these things I'm reading and trying to tell you about; the hard times make you grow, think, learn and try new things which leads to new stories. **It's all about the story.**

Countless times I've asked myself where I would be today if I had ignored my aching stomach and kept pushing with the athlete-mind I used to have. Maybe I would have ten times more followers and exposure than I have now. I probably would have a longer list of achievements on the paper, but would I be happy? Fulfilled? Would I use my talents and my potential I've been given to the fullest? Would I be one with myself, connected as a whole, following my nature?

No.

By blindly following a road without asking why every single day, you learn nothing. You become numb and you forget what it's like to live. During my time 'off' from playing I learned what it's like to have friends, what it's like to have a home, what makes my heart beat faster and what makes my heart break. I learned about other worlds outside of music and I re-experienced that fire you feel the first time you lose yourself in something. That first time you lose yourself in a song or during a gig or while playing. I re-experienced my fire through writing, through dancing, through love and through realizing that I am more than my achievements. My whole life I had built my identity on my achievements in whatever I was doing, and I thought that my only value lied in how much I could prove people wrong. I dare to say that by 'doubting' my life within music I found an identity, a personality. I got a glimpse of what life could be really about, and I felt alive for the first time in years. For the first time in my life, even. And these things, your personal journey, realizing your nature, is what makes you a good artist, and that's what this story is all about. Your journey through real life. Your discovery of your character in solitude and around other people, the moments of clarity when you feel loved and the moment when your heart breaks so much that you can hear it crack. When you run careless and free on open fields and when you're struggling on your way home on the tube. This is what makes you a real artist. Experiences, moments, stories. Falling recklessly in love, losing someone you love and then learning to belong to yourself again. Going to new places, meeting new people, driving in the middle of the night on empty streets. Going to the ocean and staying there until 6am, smoking cigarettes and talking about roses and butterflies. These are the things that will give you something worth writing about, worth singing about, worth creating art around. For so long I refused myself the simple pleasure of living, because I felt like I was wasting away, I wasn't working hard enough. But you won't find these stories by blind athlete-discipline and hours in front of your computer. I'm not saying that being disciplined and business-focused isn't important, like I've said, if it wasn't for the two years of numbing focus I wouldn't be able to do this full-time, but after a while you need to re-think and re-evaluate. What really matters for you and your heart in the end? How do you actually want to spend this time you've been given, and what do you actually want to get out of this?

While floating on this new path of mine, the path of figuring out where I wanted to go from here, I searched new worlds every single day, which made it quite hard to keep my artistic direction as a songwriter. I was introduced to new stories, new music, new opinions every single day. I discovered new books, authors, writers, dancers, history and mythologies and I found myself a little different, a little changed every single night. I've always written a lot, not music, just writings. Journals, poetry and short stories. I've always been hypnotized by dancers and their movements, and I grew a passion for old theatres, musicals, cathedrals with their mythologies and old paintings. I could spend days in different art galleries, talking to artists about what inspired them and what they wanted to get out of doing what they did.

I remember one particular day in a small town somewhere in England. I had found a small local pub the night before that seemed to be the place where all the locals went to hang, and so I managed to talk myself into getting a set the next night. During the day I went to discover the small village and found a little museum. I went in and found the most beautiful paintings, old furniture and amazing stories about them. It was one of these small museums with a dark, cosy atmosphere that makes you want to whisper and not breathe too loud. I walked around the place for some time before the man who worked there came up and asked if

I was new to the town. I told him I was just visiting and he smiled and explained that he usually recognises every single person who walks into the museum, the town was that small. I smiled and asked him about the paintings, how old they were and what they meant. He looked at me for a while, as if he was trying to decide if he could trust me or not, until he pointed at the painting in the corner, saying "That's my latest one, I painted that two weeks ago and it's a portrait of my daughter. We lost her to cancer two years ago". I was speechless. First of all it hit me, this wasn't a museum at all, it was a gallery with this man's art. He created these things with his own hands, from his own story. Real life. Second of all, when I find out that someone has experienced hurt, pain, struggle or loss in any way, I immediately fall in love with their story. I want to know more, I want to know how he felt that second he lost his daughter. Who was she, who could she have been? I want to know if he's still thinking about her right before he's falling asleep, can he still hear her laughter? Did it change him? What made him go on? I went up closer to the painting and observed the girl's face, how he had captured every line, every detail, every grain of hair, every single thing about his biggest loss. I observed her eyes, which were filled with a blue kind of beautiful sadness. Her smile, that kind of smile you give when you're trying to swallow the tears in your throat. The girl in the painting looked like around 9 years old, but she looked so wise, so real, so aware. I woke up from my daydreaming and realised that the man was observing me from the other side of the room, smiling. "Come," he said and led me into another room, where he showed me another painting, a painting of the same girl but as a baby.

I spent six hours in that gallery, listening to the man telling me the story behind each and every one of his paintings, and I realised that this is what art should be about. It should reflect your story. It should be a gallery of your heart, your life, your journey. I asked him what makes him turn to his painting, what makes him happy, what makes him sad. I asked him about his family, his daughter, his parents. Were they supportive? Did they understand his art too? What's your biggest dream and what do you want to get out of this?

An ordinary day, in the most mediocre little town, I stumbled upon the most beautiful and crucial conversation of my life, and that is what this is all about. It's about the possibilities of what can happen, of what might happen, every single day. It's about trusting the world and the universe and let it lead you to wherever you're supposed to end up. I know that my belief and spirituality only belongs to me, but I do believe that whatever you seek is seeking you. I do believe that my search for the definition of art and what it's all about led me to this conversation. I went into that museum, hoping to kill some time before my gig, and left six hours later with a completely different view on what the arts is about, what music is about, what poetry is about. I had a thousand new questions to think about and a thousand new stories to make sense of. I went to the pub that night and played the best show of my life. The sound was crap, the crowd and the people in the pub were loud and drunk (at least they bought my album and the sound-guy bought me beer to make up for the crappy sound), but I was connected. I was so connected to my music, my story, this journey I was on, and I lost myself completely in the sound. And that's how I slowly realised that I have so much more to learn, to discover, to understand and experience before I show the world what I'm about. No, actually, what I realised was that it's not about creating a finished product, as in an artist or a story or an album, and then give it to the world. It's about letting the world learn and discover and grow with you. Let them in on this journey of discovery with me. And that's how this book ended up in your hands.

I had a five-year plan, a business plan of when to release what and how to do it and I had already written the songs I wanted to have on my albums for the next three years. But in just a day it all changed. And that's what being flexible is about. I could have ignored my new realisations and kept pushing for that five-year plan, or I could choose to follow my heart and guts and listen to the signs, telling me to realise my true nature and search for something more. Because that's how I see this. I know a lot of people saw it as if I was giving up, taking a step back, slacking off. I had my old friends from back home telling me that it was about time that I realised how naive and immature I'd been. But I saw it as the start of something real, something true, something greater. The search for something more. I knew that there was so much more for me. Life was about so much more, could be so much more.

And this is when I made the choice to let go. I'd been trying to find a way to keep going, to keep pushing, to restart my fire, but this was when I realised that that time had passed. It was time to let go and start something new, completely new. And this is where the real journey starts. This is where I found the most beautiful places, lessons, people and friends. Because this when I gave up this inwardly battle. Stopped fighting against myself. When I stepped out of my own way and started the everlasting journey of building a home in my own body, my own mind, my own self. This is when I learned that if you can live with yourself, you can live anywhere in any way you want.

> You know who you are,
> you just have to believe it.
> — Elizabeth Scott

It was a very ordinary day after a little more than a year on the road, the day I arrived in London, in a not so new city and I suddenly felt at home, because I'd been there before and I knew what the train-station looked liked. It was June and I wasn't freezing for once, the warmth was refuelling every fibre of my shrinking body. The people had fled the city for the summer, so there was suddenly space for both me and my journey and I didn't have to fight for the air anymore. It was a short moment of clarity, an ordinary text message, a cheap bottle of wine, a blanket and a witnessing of the sunset in the park. It was a very ordinary thing, his hand in mine, his speeches and my silence, and I think I must have left my mind somewhere in these three hundred venues I'd been to the last three hundred days because suddenly I wasn't scared anymore. I wasn't angry or sad or ugly and I enjoyed being around other people, because I was lucky to find friends who were burning too. And I found someone who got stars in his eyes when he talked about music and he wanted more. He wanted more of everything and he was greedy and spoke ugly and beautifully and his words were messy and I just couldn't take my eyes off him. No, scratch that; I couldn't take my mind off him. It was just a very ordinary thing, his room and my worn out bag. Lying on empty streets at 5am, sharing the last cigarette, talking about oceans and leaving. Wanting more. No keys and no commitments. The open road and new beginnings every day, and how I suddenly felt seen, existent, alive. I felt understood, and I realized that my journey, the story I'd been writing, didn't mean a thing until I shared it with someone.

Once I was beautiful, now I am myself.
– Anne Sexton

Forever ago I packed my life in a bag and left my home, my family and everything I'd ever known. I bought a one-way ticket to London and started a journey that would turn out to be my life. And my life, would turn out to be everything I thought it wouldn't be. Back then I called myself a songwriter without averting my eyes. I tagged my songs with empty words about genre and style, told people without hesitation what bands I liked and what bands I didn't like and I refused to spend time on things that wouldn't lead me anywhere, and I did all this without giving it a second thought. Today, I don't call myself a songwriter. I stumble on calling myself a writer, an artist or when giving myself any other label. To define is to limit and all I really want to say with this book is that we have oceans left to sail and other worlds to see. You have universes within you yet to be discovered and you won't discover your own passions, your own nature, until you let go of the picture you've built up of yourself in your head. If you just dare to question everything you've taken for granted, you will find possibilities and new beautiful beginnings. Beginnings and new chapters you never thought could be. Today, I don't really know where I want to end up or how I want the world to see me, and I don't care because it's all about me, here and now, this very second. Can I look myself in the mirror without breaking it? Can I sit in meditation for an hour, with nothing but me and my mind and be content? There's a passage in one of my favourite novels *To the Lighthouse* by Virginia Woolf, where the main character is reflecting on her husband. He's a successful writer with so many thoughts in his head and she loves him. But when they're out walking one evening he keeps talking about his books and goals and achievements, and she thinks to herself that she is proud of her husband for being dedicated "but can he see the flowers?" Do you notice the simple pleasures of living, like the coffee in the morning with someone you love, a smile from a stranger; can you see the flowers?

I'm definitely not where I hoped I would be when it comes to my music career. When I started this I was hoping to be full-time touring with at least 2 full-length albums out by now. And if I would have fought in a different way, I could probably have been there by now, by what I've learned is that every setback, every struggle, will always lead you to the path where you're supposed to be even if it feels wrong in the beginning. I believe I'm exactly where I'm supposed to be.

You just need to trust your story.

I'm trying not to care anymore if the critics can't understand my music or if my family can't understand the life I've built, or even if my best and closest friends criticize the way I live now and how I've changed, because I found my identity. I found a home within myself where I can be me and be okay with that. Somewhere in the doubting, the questioning, the countless trains to nowhere and in the conversations with strangers, I found a way to feel home in my own mind, in my own body, with my own life. I used to dedicate my life to my achievements, to how the world saw me, but today I dedicate myself to myself. I belong to myself again and my only task is to live according to my own definition of happiness and freedom. Today, all I want is to live a life where I can be me, and be okay with that. Maybe even proud of that one day. I'm not there yet and some days I'm still struggling, because that's life and this isn't a fictional story with an ending of happily ever after.

Look, there are days when I wake up beside someone I love and I feel beautiful. The air is clean and crisp outside the window and the silence doesn't remind me of my loneliness anymore. The sweet smell of being home, beside someone you trust, and for a short moment of clarity I feel safe. Everything turned out fine. I survived after all. But know that there are days when I feel ugly and weak and if I bothered to pick up the phone and let you in, you would find me curled up in the corner on the floor with an unbearable pain in every muscle of my body because my mind tells me not to eat but to run, and I can't run from myself because I've been everywhere and nowhere and I'm still me, you see? There are days when I want to shut the fuck up and stop being so damn open about my disordered behaviour and learn how to act again, and there are days when I pass out in the shower and still can't bring myself to just fucking eat.

There are days when I couldn't care less about what all of you think about my art because this is my life and all I have. But then there are days when all I want is to be beautiful and good enough and someone to count on. Someone to like and love and believe in.

And all I really wanted to say with all this, is that this is okay. Because this is life and this is what growth is and it's not supposed to be a straight line. It's not supposed to be a straight road with no obstacles, because then it probably wouldn't lead to anything of importance, would it? It hurts because it matters and the days you're struggling are the days you're growing, learning, building your strength, and you're not supposed to run from fear, challenges, setbacks and bad weather, because these things are the things you will tell about, write about, create your story and your memories from. You have to welcome it and embrace it with all you've got and instead of running away in fear be curious about what the storm is meant to teach you. You've got to learn to turn everything into a battle because that's when you can win, when you can grow, and no one else can define that for you. You need to dedicate yourself to your own story. And the most beautiful thing is that it's all about you, and no one else has anything to do with that. It has nothing to do with degrees or universities or achievements on paper, it's all about you. **This is all about you.** Your journey and your story, so make sure you're the one who's writing it.

It was a very ordinary day, the day I realised that my becoming is my life and my home and that I don't have to do anything but trust the process, trust my story and enjoy the journey. It doesn't really matter who I've become by the finish line, the important things are the changes from this morning to when I fall asleep again, and how they happened, and who they happened with. An hour watching the stars, a coffee in the morning with someone beautiful, intelligent conversations at 5am while sharing the last cigarette. Taking trains to nowhere, walking hand in hand through foreign cities with someone you love. Oceans and poetry.

It was all very ordinary until my identity appeared, until my body and mind became one being. The day I saw the flowers and learned how to turn my daily struggles into the most extraordinary moments. Moments worth writing about. For so long I let my life slip through my fingers,
 like water.
    I'm holding on to it now
        and I'm not letting go.

JOURNALS

The diary taught me that it is in the moments of emotional crisis that human beings reveal themselves most accurately. I learned to choose the heightened moments because they are the moments of revelation.
– Anais Nin

March 4, 2012

Instant coffee and tip from the sound-guy. I'm learning sounds, laying wide awake on different sofas every night. I know the difference between a well built wall and broken strength. All my life I've been afraid of people, of making friends, getting too close to anyone, and now I'm meeting such beautiful and wise people every single day, making me doubt the way I've been living my whole life. I'm learning mindfulness, reading about gurus, poets and bibles every day on different trains to nowhere. I don't know what I'm learning but I hope I will understand one day.

I'm selling my heart with each album and a silent prayer that they'll be gentle with it, gentle with me. And then the concerned looks they throw when I point at my worn out bag and broken guitar case as the answer to where I live. Sure I could spend a year or two selling my days and time for money, and I could buy all these things people want to have without never really needing it. It's just that when I'm on that stage every night, it all just seems so stupid. My guitar, my voice, my words, my story. That's all I want, that's what makes my heart beat. What am I supposed to do with belongings and material stuff when all I want is this.

The open road and a new beginning every day.

I don't have a lot and I gave away the things you're supposed to have to be able to live. I don't own any keys and I threw my phone in the river. My family will always remember me as the confused one who left and never came back. I'm searching. I will be forever wandering. I don't know what I'm looking for, but I will spend the rest of my life trying to find it.

I don't know where I'm going, but I'm on my way.

Dec 3, 2011

This is for getting drunk instead of dealing with the real problem. This is for going home, locking the door and turning off the lights so no one knows you're there, cleaning out the closet. This is for the cigarettes that kill you and that's why you're smoking.

Here's to the life I could live, with exciting heights and free falls. New cities every day, laughter with old friends and long walks in the middle of the night with someone beautiful. The life I could have. My name is Charlotte, and that's the life I could have.

Well, this is for turning on the music so loud you can't hear the voices in your head, screaming no. This is for the phone you're turning off every morning so you don't have to talk to anyone. My name is Charlotte, and this is for the times you don't look before you cross the road.

Dec 7, 2011

There will be time for apologies.
You will need it, and I will give it to you, fallen on my knees. There will be time for explanations. Questions why I did it, what I was thinking and how I could be so careless. I won't have answers, only repeating "I'm sorry", and you will go back and forth from the door, unable to place your feelings. You won't know if you forgive me or if you no longer can look me in the eyes.

I am the contrast. I am forever the crack in the window that lets the winter in. I am forever the moment between laughter and tears, happiness and sadness. I am light and darkness. I am fire and ice. You will try to take me into your life, but I won't fit, and you will not know how to tell me

that there is simply no place for me.

There is simply no place for a girl like me.

Feb 3, 2012

The best conversations are held at 4am, laying on the ground with no intention of getting up.

We drove for an hour on empty streets with no eyes in the rear view. Gas station coffee, cheap whiskey and smoking through the window. You told me that you could never do this with anyone else, that this is wrong, irresponsible, not grown up behaviour. You went quiet for a while, as if you were discussing with yourself, arguing, pros and cons. I kept my eyes on the moon, lit a cigarette and then you said,

"but with you all this makes sense. With you everything that usually makes sense, doesn't make sense at all anymore. And all this, that usually doesn't make sense, suddenly does, you know?".

I've never felt so weightless.

We drove to the ocean and smoked cigarettes until six in the morning when I fell asleep on your chest.

When you woke up I was gone and you went back to your sense-making behaviour and I keep having my best conversations while the world is asleep, trying to identify my own existence, or find the definition of being me somewhere between dawn and the sunrise.

Dear universe, may I never find myself.

Feb 20, 2012

I am done with my childish safety in sorrow. I no longer wrap myself in its cold embrace. I know life, not enough, but enough to know life. I am not here to spend another second wishing for salvation or change. I was not born to be a skeleton. I no longer wish for rain on sunny days, neither do I wish for sun on rainy days. I no longer wish for everlasting love and forever. No, give me change, throw me new battles, new mountains, new views and make them change me. For things that matter end up changing you. May I never go to sleep as the same person I was the morning before, because that would mean I just wasted a day of my life. A day of exploring, journeying, learning, training. A day of wandering, books, music, poetry, laughter, natural ecstasy, adrenaline.

Tonight I will get rid of this dead skin. I want to blind people with my very flesh. I want my existence to be something worth writing about.

Let my existence be something worth writing about.

To you. Yes you.

You're always my concern.
You have built a comfortable home in my sadness and I understand if you don't want to leave. I can see that you're not happy, but you're smiling and that hurts even more than if you cried. I wish I could make your world appear a little better, a little easier, but I can't and you're not here and I can't even hold your hand and tell you to hold your head up. I don't have any answers to give you and I can't make this raining stop. All I have is my words and my voice and if that's the only thing I can do to tell you that you're not alone, then that's what I am going to do.

Following the heroes.

I am broken nerves.

I am signals from the brain to the muscles, trying to reach out, create a movement, a sign of aliveness.

Screaming but can't really be heard.

I am the first glimpse of the sun after a long and cold winter. The first green tree, the first flower to blossom, the first bird to sing in the spring.

I am also the first tree to let go of my leaves and colours and give in for the cold. The first flower to go back to my hiding, the first bird to leave as soon as it gets cold. Safe from violence and ugliness, far, far away.

Still I embrace the rain like no one else and I call for storms because I live for the moments when I get through to the other side with all my organs intact.

I change with the seasons and the seasons live in me, depending on the weather as if it's something to be trusted. I don't feel safe unless I'm far below or high above, near the ocean, or climbing the mountain. Where I can't be reached or seen by anyone or anything and not even myself, because it seems to me that these voices in my head get louder just to kill the noise from the outside,

and so I need to go away from time to time.

You will never see me surrender, never see me cry, but you will often see me walk away. Turn around and just leave, without looking back. Detachment from myself to observe my own

solitude.

I've been studying myself like a scientist, trying to find some kind of proof to my worthiness. And I should get a degree in self-observation because I know every inch of my own being and I know the answer to all the questions

of the universe but still
I stumble on my own name.
So tell me lord or God or whatever spirit there is up there, where do you want me to go from here? Because it seems to me that human beings should love themselves and I can't even touch my own skin. I'm reading bibles and poetry, astronomy and Zen, and they're all telling me that love is the answer. Love thyself and love the earth and the people around you, and beauty shall be found. So simple.
So damn simple.

So they gave me love in form of poison and tiny little pills, programming my emotions, teaching me how to feel. To act correct and talk correct and answer without knowing the question, because that, my dear, is how you get love. Yes that, dear youth, is how you'll be loved. I tried to medicate my own fucked up little mind with chemicals and adrenaline, tasting sweeter every night, shaking louder every time. Sitting wide awake in bed until the world disappears, writing poetry to concentrate on something real while waiting for the love to arrive.
I've been looking for it night after night, waiting patiently for it to show up, maybe somewhere in between the state of awake and asleep, alive and not so alive, sober and not so sober.
(I lost track of the difference somewhere in between.)

I need the stars and the moon and the dark and the night, because I find it hard to come alive when the sun is up, when the world exists, when the people talk and walk and just simply are. I need nature and my nature is what I'm searching and I'm prepared to follow comets and myths and every single God there is to find it. I'm prepared to swallow fire and memorise all the 366 sonnets by Petrarch or meditate with Siddhartha for six years, because I'm following my nature and it tells me to keep wandering, because wandering is what I know and I'm pretty damn good at it.

I'm following the heroes and I'm learning
  how to stand up
    on my own.
I'm following the stars for my reasons and every night
  I hear them calling me,
    telling me to keep walking
      on my own.

    I'll be walking on my own.

March 23, 2012

Lately I've been stuck in a form of non-being; I have nothing left to feel. I went to the ocean today, just in time to witness the sun disappear, where the sky touches the sea. I put my right hand on my chest, trying to find my heartbeat. Somewhere deep under this dry skin, is there any life?

It was so quiet, not even the ocean made a sound. "Dear old heart, are you still there? Why are you so quiet?" I sat there for a long time, until I decided that my heart wouldn't find anything to beat for in this place.

On my way home I was just about to cross the street when I saw this car driving way too fast by the end of the road, so I stopped and took a second to wonder where the driver was going, and why he was in such a hurry.

I stopped.

The cyclist behind me didn't.

Ten minutes later there were ambulances screaming but I couldn't hear a thing. Blue light flickering somewhere far away but still right in front of my eyes.

People running everywhere but nowhere.

My heart has never beaten so fast.
I swear, I even held it in my hand.

April 13, 2012

It's like one of these summer nights with your friends by the ocean. You're drinking straight from the bottle, singing the memories of the best years and for just that night you're infinite. You're exactly where you're supposed to be. There is no future. You have earned the present.

And I'm taking trains to nowhere, hoping to be able to hold on to these few moments on stage every night. And I'm thinking that I'm me,

and this very moment,

I'm okay with that.

June 12, 2012

There are very few friends that will lie down with you on empty streets in the middle of the night, without a word. No questions, no asking why, just quietly lay there with you, observing the stars, until you're ready to get back up on your feet again and walk the last bit home, softly holding your hand as a quiet way of saying "I'm here".

It was a beautiful night.

June 14, 2012

There is nothing sweeter than hearing your voice after a long day in this city. But my voice is sore and my insides empty and I have nothing more to give. Winter's coming soon and love is not enough. The hotel room is empty and every trace of you is gone.

I will be sorry every day of my life.

June 16, 2012

Today I witnessed the way a heart shatters. I witnessed the way a life breaks. You think you're so wise and you think you know anything about life, until you're thrown right in the middle of it - face to face with existence. I write all these big words about life and death and searching as if I knew, but then when it came to it - I was speechless. I didn't know what to say. I wanted to be able to say all these things that I've figured out the last years. All these things about the fact that living doesn't have to be according to the system, the society's system with rules and timelines. I wanted to say all these things about how you just have to hold on to the things you love and let go of all the rest. But I couldn't say a thing. Empty words with no meaning, slowly putting away the vodka bottle. Throwing the pills in the garbage. Try to breathe, stay calm, be the hero you've been looking for yourself your whole life. But I'm too god damn caught up in my own head to pull myself together to say anything that matters at all and I just really wish you knew how much you would kill me if you disappeared. I've spent my life detaching myself from society, my family and my friends but you broke down my walls and now I need you. I don't know how to exist if you disappear.

I want to sleep for a thousand years,
    but I can't even close my eyes.

June 17, 2012

~~.. x~~ ~~xxx~~ Today I felt nothing at all.

Learning Fire.
You love, You burn

July 8, 2012

This morning I woke up before the alarm clock went off and the sky outside was a big red ocean. You're beautiful when you're sleeping so I spent an hour observing the way you breathe. Inhale, exhale, without a thought of tomorrow. The window was open and the air was so crisp and I couldn't imagine how to ever ask for more than this.

July 14, 2012

You're making me revalue and rearrange. It's not that hard anymore. I used to want so much; I wanted it all. The world or nothing. It was all a long process of becoming. Becoming something better and more accepted. But you're teaching me beauty. With you, there are no ordinary moments.

I used to want so much. It's not that hard anymore. Give me star-filled nights, intelligent conversations and new songs to write. Let me wake up next to you, have coffee in the morning and wander through the city with your hand in mine, and I'll be happy for the rest of my fucked up little life.

July 15, 2012

My favourite place in all the world is next to you.

July 16, 2012

You're all I want to know.

I want to be consumed and destroyed by your mind, your screwed up little thoughts. I want to memorise the distance between each of your ribs and then learn your anatomy the same way a traveller knows his map.

I want to disappear in your existence to forget about my own. Forget about my body, the way I can make it change but still I feel the same. Forget about my ghost and shadow and this inwardly behaviour I can't seem to learn.

Now I will forget, everything I've ever learned.

You're all I want to know.

July 18, 2012

My favourite part is to observe your eyes when you're trying to understand something I've just said. I know my words don't always make sense, but I love how you're really trying to figure me out.

In fact, I like to observe your eyes at anytime.

July 25, 2012

I was following storms and destruction and you were the calmness I'd forgotten. I didn't know a place like that could exist and now that you're gone I'm left wondering if it really happened. Can life really be that simple? And maybe life isn't supposed to be this hard after all? Maybe we're just really good at complicating things when it's really fucking simple.

With your hand in mine I could cross oceans. I could move mountains and nothing was impossible. For the first time in forever I wasn't scared, and now that I've experienced the opposite there's no way I can go back.

Every second is a countdown to when I will see you again.

July 29, 2012

I wish I would have had done so much more with you.

My greatest regrets are the early goodbyes. The times I let go a second too early from your hand. The times I averted my eyes when you tried to capture it. How I never held you long enough. The mistake of thinking about meaningless melancholy while laying beside you in bed, staring at the ceiling. I wish I would have done so much more with you.

I wish we had gone to more parks. Found more four-leaf clovers. I wish we had stayed up every night until our eyes were so heavy that we fell asleep on each other. I wish we had been young enough to take random trains to nowhere every single day, just to experience each other in as many situations and places as possible.

My sadness lies in the fact that we weren't done yet, we never even started. We never even got the chance to lift from the ground. We weren't done with the waking up next to each other. The experiencing of energy, fires, explosions,

comets.

I thought I wanted more time, but all I really wanted was to experience every little piece of you

while I had you.

My greatest regrets are the early goodbyes.

August 2, 2012

My heart was racing every time you came near.

It's very quiet now.

It's mostly still.

August 4, 2012, *Searching for myself in Edinburgh.*

This is the part when I realise that I too need to learn from my writings. I too need to be brave and strong and go on even though it would be so much easier to step out into this rain and lay there until someone was forced to drive all the way up here and take me home. This is the part when I will do the bravest thing in my whole life - I will take a breath, and then another, and I will go on living.

I will choose to be happy because I got to know someone who showed me fire again, not sad because I lost him. Because that's what you do when you've experienced beauty. You go out there and you search for it again, again and again, even more determined to reach your highest potential. Now you know that a higher place can be reached. You've seen it in someone else, but it's up to you to find it in yourself. You fight and lose and love again, and you learn from it every time.

That's what this is about.

That's the only good fight there is.

August 6, 2012

It's like a stomach-ache after not eating for five days. The muscles are starting to eat themselves,

and you couldn't care less.

It's about holding on to every moment with every ounce of your being, every atom. It's about memorising every expression, the way your muscles work, the way you speak, how your voice sounds during every part of the day. It's about not feeling the goodbye in every kiss, in every hug, in every touch. It's about trying to keep your voice steady even with a knife in your throat.

It's August and I'm tired of being strong.

I never really was very brave.

Throw me on sharp edges, I've never felt so destructive.

August 8, 2012

There is nothing more beautiful than talking to you after a long day in this city. I try to picture your face as I read your words, how you talk with your hands when you're trying to make a point, how you drag your feet when you're tired and how your eyes are burning when you truly believe in something (you showed me fire again). How you smoke your cigarette, how you disappear when the music starts and how your hand fits perfectly in mine. How we slept with the window open and how sweet the rain sounded in the morning. Nothing was impossible with you and now that you're not here even the simple things are too much effort.

I'm seeing all these new places, meeting all these new people, but all I can think of is you.

I could travel the world and not let go,

You're shaping me, and I have no regrets.

Kiss me like you mean it, one last time.

August 9, 2012

It's 4.30 am again and I can't decide if it's hunger pains or just the loneliness coming back. It was a beautiful evening with big sweaters, wine and the light you only get during summer. But then it got dark and I stared at my empty bed for two hours before I decided to sleep on the floor

(I wish you were here).

The way everything is more intense during night makes the catastrophe of my personality pulsate wilder in my veins and it's getting to the point where I'd like to put a needle in them, deep down just to see what sort of ghosts I have in there that makes it so damn hard to be still. To go to rest.

It's a longing to live on the open road with my guitar and best friends, and at the same time move far into the woods, live in a cabin and never have my life in bags again. It's a longing to love so recklessly that the world will laugh at us, at the same time I'd like to cut all the ropes and never come back.

It's 5 am now and I can't decide if it's really late or really early. If the day is ending or starting. If I'm falling or flying. If I'm still drunk or hung over.

I can't decide if it's just hunger pains, or the loneliness coming back.

August 11, 2012

It's not that hard. It's really fucking simple. It was raining the whole day until I saw you and by the second you took my hand the sun was shining. "You're way too attached to your melancholy" they've told me, and I never really understood until now. If you find happiness and everything you've ever asked for, you take it. You thank the Gods and the spirits and every atom in the universe for all the crooked roads and misguided nights because they led you here, to this very moment. You take care of it and make sure that you never ever take it for granted.

If you find happiness so beautiful that your heart is racing, you take it, you don't give it away,
                and you don't fucking leave.

Alone in a room full of people.

. . . and he took her hand and lead her away from the crowd, away from the city, away from the streetlights. Away from commitment, expectations of being, the drunken youth. Empty streets and no questions. They walked in silence, for silence is what she knows and that's when she speaks the most.

August 12, 2012

It rained today.

I stayed in bed for 2 hours, pretending to hear you breathe. I fell asleep and rolled around to take your hand, then I woke up and decided to sleep on the floor from now on.

(Every time I wake up and you're not here, I die a little more inside)

I touched my skin where your hands used to live, feeling the echo of your fingerprints. I decided to never shower again.

After four cups of coffee I noticed my hands were shaking just like yours always did. I smashed the last cup on the floor.

The pieces are still there.

I went for a walk in the city to find something to think about or someone new to talk to, but the streets were suddenly empty and all the people gone. And walking through cities is not the same without holding your hand anyway.

By lunch it was still raining. I was still not hungry.

I decided to use my sorrow for what I'm here for, so I took my guitar and a notebook and placed myself on the floor, deciding to pick myself up and write my heart out, the music that can take me far far far away from here.

Every line is about you.

By afternoon I got dizzy and tried to remember when I last ate. I couldn't remember.

I went to the food store to buy a salad, but everything involved cucumber. I decided to never eat again.

By the time the darkness came I panicked, threw your t-shirt in the trash (I'm sorry) and tried to wash away every trace of you on my shrinking body. I scrubbed and scrubbed and scrubbed until my hands were bleeding.

I can still feel you.

It's still raining.
I'm deciding to not sleep again until I know I'll wake up beside you.
Or until it won't hurt to wake up.

August 18, 2012 – La Vita Nuova.
I'm packing my life in a bag again, saying goodbye and writing the last letters. It's been a long journey, back and forth, hide and seek, but this time it's different. This time I am different. I'm not sure where I want to end up this time, but I know how to get there, or at least the first direction, the first turn, the first sunset. I'm longing for peace. I'm longing for borrowed guitars and detachment. Horizons, cheap whiskey straight from the bottle
and your hands in mine.

August 25, 2012
"I wish I could spend more life with you."

It's a simple word in the most ordinary sentence that makes my heart beat a little faster. It's the way you sometimes choose a word that no one else would ever choose, the way you speak, that makes me stop for half a second and cling to it.
Life is time and time is all there is and I promise I will learn, I'll be learning you patiently.

I will learn all these things I should have learned while I was busy running away from the life I'd been given. I want to know how you handle lost luggage, tangled Christmas lights and broken mirrors. I want to know how you speak when someone offends you - do you keep calm or do raise your voice? I want to know what you do when your friends are sad, what you say when someone gets something you've been fighting for yourself and if you get jealous? Have you ever hit someone?
I have. How does that make you feel?

I will learn to be something you can need,
I promise I'll be learning you patiently.

August 28, 2012
It's still raining. I'm deciding to not sleep again until I know I'll wake up beside you.
(Sometimes I can still feel you in the dark)

September 1, 2012

It's like the text-message in the morning, the first thing I think about when I open my eyes. You write good morning and call me beautiful and that's enough to turn the most rainy day into something poetic and calm.

My blood runs smoother and my nerves function better. I didn't sing for weeks and now I find myself singing my heart out in the shower again. These words appear as natural as I breathe and I don't hide my body under ten layers of clothes anymore.

You write and tell me about the beauty of the sky at 6am on an ordinary weekday and that's what I'm trying to tell you. For me,

you're the beauty of the sky at 6am on an ordinary weekday.

September 5, 2012

I need to do some serious cleaning of my closet. I can't sleep because I can't stand the things I dream about. I panic when your hands get too close because it's pushing the button of flashbacks and I can't fucking turn it off. I'm way too old to build a comfort in hunger and I want to get over this crap now. I held on to it so long because it was my safety, it was my tragedy and no one could take it away from me. But I've found something and someone who's worth fighting for. Something better to hold on to.

I'm ready to free myself from these chains now.

I will be free now.

September 6, 2012

My heart was racing so fast back then, back then when you were around. Sometimes I had to stop and rest, calm it down. *"Inhale, exhale, where are you trying to run?"* But now it's mostly quiet. Now it's mostly still.

Some nights I lie awake, trying to convince it to not give in, to keep beating through the night even if I fall asleep. *"Just a little longer, please? In the morning I'll take better care of you, I promise, just let me sleep for some hours.*

Stay with me. . . ?"

But it's getting colder and winter's coming soon and my heart can't seem to fit in between my ribs anymore. It never made a lot of sound, never had a lot of life, but then you came along and now your fingerprints are echoing in the emptiness and my tired little heart can't seem to find peace. Its constant craving for something it can't have.

Some nights it's crying so loud I can hear it break.

Sep 8, 2012

I can't eat, I can't sleep and I feel myself fading with every passing hour. I'm exhausted and my head is cloudy and I see myself disappearing every time I cross a road. I don't want to go on like this, I want to get out. I'm back to coming up with bad excuses for not seeing my friends and I hate myself for pushing people away again, for spending my days with the door closed, again.

Teach me how to live, day by day, because I've tried every way I can think of and nothing seems to work.

Sep 10, 2012

It's work and it's money and it's just too many people acting like stones around here, walking without bending their knees, without rolling their feet. It's insomnia and colder weather and I'm never really hungry, but never really full. But then there's you and the way you smile that makes me take in a little more air in every breath. There's you and your eyes and the way you talk as if you're carrying all the secrets of the world, makes me think that maybe this place isn't so hopeless after all, not so lifeless - after all.

I've been clinging to the darkness, because that's where you find exploding fires, falling stars and wishes with hope. But the darkness is nothing compared to your eyes and - oh sweet magic, they fulfil my wishes before I even make them. They give me answers before I ask the questions, know the questions.

There are stars in your eyes darling, there's a fire in your heart.   And you don't even know.

Sep 13, 2012

And so tonight I will tear down the moon because it doesn't mean a thing when it's not reflected in your eyes. It's just empty light, hurting my sight. And then I will rip the curtains down and stare through the window, because now the night is reflecting me and you and I - it could be so beautiful with the stars and the moon and the quiet. But if one element is missing, it's just a dark black hole of nothingness, and I will be staring into the lack of light until I fall asleep, and maybe when I wake up it'll still be dark, and then I will do it all over again until you come and give the moon back its meaning.
Can't you see, there are no stars here when you're away. They live in your eyes darling.

Sep 17, 2012

Our first assignment was a personal essay, a memoir, and I who have been everywhere and nowhere could not find a single memory worth telling. I spent days and nights staring at the blank page, searching the deepest corners of my mind: who have I been, what have I seen, what did I learn? I thought about all the nights I've spent outside, all the times I laid down to cry and how I took a deep breath every morning and decided to simply go on. Because what else is there to do? Decide that this is it?

I quit, I'm done?

Oh if I could find words to justify those feelings I've carried. I could write the thickest of books with explosions of emotions from a young girl's lost heart. I could make you see, make you hear, make you feel, at least a tiny fragment

of what's out there.

But I'm coming to the conclusion that there are no such words, and if I can't make you understand completely, if I can't make you feel it, live it, taste it - I'd rather leave it unspoken.

And so I, who thought I carried the possibilities to be the voice of my people and write down the story of my life, failed my first assignment and handed in 6 blank pages with the title:

"This is the start, the rest is up to you."

School was just never meant for me,
I never fit in and I never stood out
I'm done with having my art judged
x xx   xx I never really was very brave

Sep 26, 2012

I never have time to write anymore. And when I do I only write about how I never have time. It's work and it's money and I've written more lists than songs lately. I stay up all night to do all these things I need to do, be all these things I want to be, playing with shadows in the darkness that shouldn't be able to exist. Empty bottles and cigarettes while watching the sunrise, why do I complain? I have it all, everything I ever asked for. I wanted distraction and I got it. It's just a mind aware of the possibilities in my heart and it's triggering my destruction.

Destruction, the art of destroying.

I'm fucking tired of people throwing their dirty empty words about my so called change and can't they just let me be? My disordered mind is my best friend and eating isn't getting too complicated - it always has been and when was it ever easy? What is normal anyway? I'm addicted to the dizziness, the emptiness. That's where I keep my art, where I build my art, where I find myself. Over and over again. So don't come here thinking you can tell me something about myself that I don't already know, I'm fucking living with myself, and you think I'm not aware of my own little screwed up mind?

It's 4am again and I'm just getting started. People are boring and I want to burn with excitement or anger and bleed, bleed through my words. I want to get all fucked up and write real and raw and ugly and beautifully. I bet you're sleeping safe and calm, and you can stay there, it's safer there, and you wouldn't stand one night on this journey my mind wanders off to every night you close your eyes. I'll stay here one day and I will never come down.

I promise I can fly before I hit the ground.

It doesn't even hurt anymore.

xxx xx   I swear, it doesn't hurt.

Oct 8, 2012

5.57am and I'm finishing the last poem to the taste of the last cigarette. Smoke in my lungs, poetry on the paper. Inhale, exhale, it doesn't get much easier. I heard them say goodnight seven hours ago and in three minutes I will hear them click snooze three times before they fill the kitchen like zombies, dead people, eating dead meat with their eyes shut.

I sneak in and up the stairs, into my bed, under the blanket. Curtains to delay the start of a new day - I'm not done with this one yet. There are still things I need to do. Still things I need to say, need to be, need to feel.

But we're never really done, are we?

I watch them through my window every morning, observing as they walk with heavy steps down the street. Clean costumes with no trace of identity. All marks of a past or a future, dreams or visions are cleaned and carefully hidden away. Nine hours later I watch them stumble in through the door again, straight to the kitchen like zombies, dead people, eating dead meat with their eyes shut. I observe as they half-sleep in front of the TV, one beer, two beers, what the heck why not a whiskey. Then it gets dark and they stumble to bed, alone, often drunk, and I make my way to the front porch, getting ready to inhale smoke, exhale poetry.

And this is how we live. This is how we get by, holding on to ourselves best we can. Who says I'm using my time better than they do? We're all just trying be alive, feel alive, and who knows what that means?

It's just a bit struggle-some to see through the dark when it's October again and I'm not done with today, or yesterday, or the day before that or the year before the last one, and I wish I had more time but time is all there is and who am I to complain? I'm just 21, what do I know about the passage of time?

Let's repeat; What do I know about the passage of time?
Let's repeat; the passage of time.
We could go on like this for years.
      x xx   *Unless you find a way out.*
We're all just trying to get by.

Oct 11, 2012 – *Lost is Sweden, a place I called my home.*
It's Thursday and I'm back to where I started. Walking the same old roads, leading to the same old places. You tell yourself you've changed, you're stronger, wiser, smarter, but this place turns me into a ghost of who I really am. Or who I once was, or whatever, I'm sick and tired of coming back here and please dear life, don't make me come here again.

I saw my therapist; she valued my mind, long complicated words added to my journal, the story of my life. They know it all, they have it all written down, carefully analysed. My fucked up little mind leaving marks on my body equals long complicated words in a journal. Sometimes I wish I could open that damned book for the world to see, throw it from the Eiffel Tower -*"Here you have the truth! Take it, I don't want it! I can't keep it any longer anyway, can't you see? It's breaking out, the cracks on my skin, escaping. Make what you want of it!"* but I never really was very brave, so I keep still, sitting in that clean room, politely answering the questions. *"Yes, maybe, no sir I don't want to die, no I'm not angry anymore, thank you."*

It's a skill you know, how to act the way people want you to act. It takes practice, and I'm a professional. Sharpened my knives for years and I know what they want to hear.

On my way back I passed that same old spot again, dragging me in like a spider and it's web. If a place can become your identity, that place will always be me.

Dear life, please don't ever make me come back here.

Oct 16 2012

It was one of these cold October days when the light makes you never want to go inside. And as the sun settled over the chimneys that night, I felt my heart change with every heartbeat. I slowly walked home alone, knowing that I was changing, that very day, that very moment. It made me both scared and excited for tomorrow. Who would I be, what would happen now? For the first time in a long time, I actually wanted to stick around to see what this world could offer,

and who I could be.

Oct 22, 2012

The heat finally left space for breathing and crisp air. The trees undressed and coloured the streets and I found myself changing with the season. I badly wanted to be that force of nature, that fire no one can touch, but I was tired. Tired, tired, tired, of being me and if I had one inch of energy to be something beautiful, I would have, but all I could care about was to make it home before it got dark.

Oct 24, 2012

"I feel ugly" I said and you looked at me as if I spoke a different language. There are things you will never understand and if there were words to describe the rapture that takes place in my head from time to time I would put my hand in front of your eyes to protect you from all the ugliness in the world.

I kept my eyes on the streetlights outside the window and you kissed every inch of my body as if you could kiss the pain away.

Memory of an early morning in December.

That morning the first snow fell and we stayed quietly in bed, watching the world turn into a thick layer of cold. Breathing in the silence that the snow brings, the compressed atmosphere, as if the whole town stayed in bed that morning. You held my hand in that way I fell in love with, not too tight but firm enough to say "I'm here and I'm not going anywhere."

I always had a feeling you knew, you just knew. Knew when I needed to hear that I wasn't alone, knew when to say my name to stop me from drifting away in my head, and most importantly - knew when to leave me alone.

You smoked another cigarette and we shared another coffee and it was just another morning that made me realise that this is all it takes to be happy.

Oct 26, 2012, *An early morning letter.*

As I was leaving the house this morning everything still felt so beautiful. I kicked the leaves on the ground and I couldn't stop smiling to myself. Not even the morning rush on the tube bothered me and I kept seeing your face in my head. When I woke you up and said I was leaving and you just opened your eyes and right away kissed me. The second you woke up, as if it was the most natural thing in the world, as if there was nothing else you could have done, or should have done. And it's just such a small action that is so easily forgotten, but I couldn't stop thinking about how beautiful it was and I was suddenly so excited for the life I've built for myself. How all these years of struggling, trying to become, suddenly lead me to this. All the beautiful things my life suddenly consists of and how I finally felt content.

I got home and it really felt like being home; I felt at home for the first time in my life. Not only in this town but in my own skin and what my existence consists of. I took the long way through the park, breathing deep, filling every fibre of my being with pureness. I felt alive with the sky and the light and the leaves on the ground, and I was still all warm and happy.

But then I don't know what happened. Like I'm always balancing between this great happiness and this unbearable sadness, and the sadness just kind of consumed me and then I thought of how I will wake up alone tomorrow again, like I did my whole life before I met you, and I told myself that maybe things aren't that different after all. Maybe you're just a better version of reality made up in my head. I have a way of changing the reality in my head and that's why I never seemed to fit. It all just felt very wrong and sad and life suddenly felt so unsure. So unbalanced and I felt it slip through my fingers again, like water.

I tried to distract myself with work and then I went for a run, hoping it would clean my head, but it didn't disappear. The sadness wouldn't disappear. So I took my guitar and decided to write and lose myself in that way that you're always talking about and it kind of just cleaned me. While writing, my head just felt so much clearer and I suddenly realized how this is what it's supposed to be like. This is what it's all about. It's about knowing that everything you ever have, every moment, every material thing, will pass and you will lose it, and there's nothing you can do about it. All you can do is close your eyes and live it, feel it, smell it, taste it as much as you can while you have it, and then never look back. And not even forward because all you will ever have is here and now, and that's where you have to be.

I need to stop seeing sadness in things that are beautiful, and realise that the happiness will always make up for the sadness, and I don't really know what I wanted to say or why I wrote this to you but I just really need you to know that I know I'm weird sometimes and that I rarely find the right words, but you make me feel better in my own skin than I've ever done. You make me feel better with my own life, like I actually want to hold on to it. I want to hold on to my life and I've never felt that before.

I never cared if I got hit by a car tomorrow morning, but you make me want to hold on.

I will hold on.

November 2, 2012

Waking up at 5am because that's when it hurts the most. Open windows and pure air, cleaning my lungs. Watching the sun rise from far away over the roofs, but it's not enough. Nothing is ever enough.

I'm still craving the emptiness, the hunger pains, the dizziness. I'm an addict and I can't get enough. I was seeking adrenaline in sharp edges, in my childish way to love, in my old habits of running away, but it doesn't match up. I always return to my safe home,

counting my bones.

There were nights in the beginning when my body still wasn't used to the natural ecstasy. I laid wide awake at 4am, strumming my fingers,

shaking from adrenaline.

Now it's just the emptiness, the lack of life.

Let me out.

Nov 28, 2012

I'd like to study myself around you because I find it quite astonishing what you do to me. I'd like the old me to witness how I spent hours just observing your breathing, as if you were breathing for me. Inhale my strength, exhale my sadness, inhale my safety, exhale my weakness.

You're like the air on a crisp winter morning, making me breathe deeper and purer, filling every fibre of my being with aliveness. It's about energy, mindfulness, just scientific health and well-being.

I was stressed and scared and I had to hurry to be someone, become something, do something. I was running and talking and cursed myself when I wasted my time on things that wouldn't get me anywhere. It was work and it was money and I was never where I was, always somewhere else in my head far, far away. And so now I'd like the old me to study the new me because I find it quite breathtaking what you do to me.

Like yesterday.

It was dark and cold and my head was blurry from days of emptiness and normally I would have distracted myself with work and destruction. Harmful behaviour from a harmful mind. But then there was you and the way you made your home in my bed and how you spent the day breathing safety into my room, without even knowing. I sat there for hours, feeling your existence filling my being with comfort, and you didn't even have to open your eyes to make me feel safe.

Heard.   Loved.

You're gone now and my bed is empty but you've left your trace of existence here, and that's enough to make me want to hold on to whatever there is to hold on to. You left your smell here and that's enough to make me put down this knife, give up on destruction and instead peacefully sit down and write. (because you've said that you like when I write and so that's what I want to do.)

You're talking about art and beauty and the definition of an artist, and the way you're creating me is the purest form, the highest level of art.

You're the artist and I'm your canvas, and if we stick together I believe we can be quite astonishing.

I believe we can be quite astonishing.

I believe you're quite astonishing.

Dec 1, 2012

And you walk away with your glory and pride
    and I sit here spitting words and wisdom
    and I curse myself but you
    even more
    with your glory and pride and you own so much and know
    so much and
what will it take to be able to stand like them, to walk
    like them?
Because I keep breaking my own feet every time I
    walk too straight,
I crack my bones every time I bend my knees
    and so now I'm sitting on the ground
    spitting words and curses and oh Mr. "know-it-all"
Because I don't see what they see and they never saw
    what I see
and how am I supposed to please anyone or anything when
everything I've ever loved I have loved alone and I run with
the speed of a child to show you what I just wrote, what I
just created, what I just painted,
    but you, with your glory and pride just laugh because you
don't see what I see and I never wanted to see the world in
the way that you see
    the world
because that's just not where I want to live, where I
        belong,
And the Gods and the damned only know where that is.
    But I'm building my own world, I'm building my own
home you see,
    and for the first time I've found someone I think I want to
have in this world.

    I'd like you to be a part of this, because I think we can live
quite beautifully here. With the small talk at night and hands
in the morning and coffee and too many cigarettes, and we

could maybe let each other know that we're not alone.
    You could let me know that I'm not alone
and I would run to meet you in your world in the middle
of any night
        if you asked me to
because I think you're quite astonishing and I think my
world might not be as beautiful without you and I think we
could be quite strange and unusual and simply extraordinary
    here.

But then there's the humans, the god damn mortals and
their stupid pride and empty words like fists thrown around
to define their class, to justify their worth and can't you see
you don't have to bother to convince me of your higher class
because I threw my worthiness and self-respect in the ocean
when I was still young enough to believe in suicide, so don't
come here and think you can bring me down because I
define my own lows. I define my own worth and you can't
do anything about it because I never wanted you in my
world anyway and so now I'm closing the door,
I'm locking the windows because I've had enough.
    I've had enough of people who I never invited walking in
to my world as if they knew anything about my mind and
my sorrow and can't you see you're not wanted here.
    Get away, get away, get away from me
    and let me be whoever I want to be
        just like I will let you be
            whatever you choose to be.

Dec 7, 2012
　　Shifting my weight for 10 minutes.
　Delaying the unbearable excitement of what will come,
what will happen, will I get out?

　It's Friday and it's getting dark again and my mind is
working overtime, overtime from all the Greek tragedies I'm
reading these nights, all the novels and poems and essays, the
old classics you're supposed to have read
　　　　　to call yourself wise.
You can quiz me on Petrarch, Medea, Shakespeare or
Dante, I know them all, and I'm sorry but they've all gone
wrong. Dumb glorified men, writing words about love and
life as if they knew. As far as I'm concerned they didn't make
it out alive either, so I'm sure as hell not going to go to them
for advice.
　And love isn't a Sunday morning with roses and wine. It's
the stealing of your breath and insecurities and uncertainty
and it hurts and I'm scared but still, still I've read Rumi's
Book of Love ten times over and I think I'm falling in love
with love a little more every time because it makes my heart
beat.
It makes my blood flow and I don't feel like throwing myself
out of the nearest window, anymore,
　at least not right now, tonight.
It's something about the constellation of certain thoughts,
certain words, certain syllables,
and it just explodes right off the page and makes its way to
my chest and kind of just finds its home there.
　It's like the filling of this great void I've carried inside for
so long.

　So I'm reading, because that's what you have to do,
and I search for myself between the lines, the definition of

what it means to me, or at least where to start looking
because I've looked everywhere real
and I'm nowhere to be found,
   so I thought I'd give this a try.
Or actually that's the only thing I can do, because I'm tired
of going everywhere and nowhere, looking for something I
don't know what it is, and I think it's actually right here, in
me, somewhere under all this dead skin. I think I've travelled
too far and too fast,
   when the answers are all within.
   When the greatest journey is under my eyelids.

So I will keep throwing off this weight, getting rid of
whatever stands between me and my insides, because I need
to get to my bones. My time is running and I need to find the
answers,
   or at least the right question.
I've been looking up, aiming for the point of your finger, but
I forgot to reach for what your finger was pointing at.
   I stopped too early.

   So, I'm reading, and I hope that other people do too.
To teach yourself. To learn yourself.
Or, actually just because I wish for someone to share some
thoughts with,
some thoughts I have on Franz Kafka and his father's lack of
belief in his talent, because I, Charlotte Eriksson, can relate.
Or maybe we could lay awake at 6am and talk about the
possibility of star-crossed lovers and if Phaedra should have
kept quiet about her love for Hippolytus or if you too could
have murdered someone because he no longer loved you
back, like Medea, because I, Charlotte Eriksson, can relate.
   Or maybe we can drive to the ocean and figure out why
Hamlet couldn't kill his father's murderer. Was he scared?

Was he dumb or too wise? Or why Dante never reached out to Beatrice because maybe they were star-crossed, meant to be, predestined.

Maybe they were meant to make each other's time disappear and burn from the way only lovers can look at each other, leaving scars in form of fingerprints, whispering comfort like only spiritual passion can.

But then again, would he be able to write all these beautiful lines if it wasn't for the unbearable longing for her, for something real.

For someone true.

The dream and the possibility of real, spiritual love?

And how everything is more magic
   when you don't know if it's real.

Until then, I will keep reading,

I stumble home like the drunk I've become. Closing the door with the darkness inside, counting my bones to make sure they're still there, that I am still here, and until I figure out what I'm supposed to do with this potential I've been given, I will keep reading,

and I will keep throwing off this weight

   To get to the inside.

My insides.

An ordinary Sunday

It was Sunday - not a day, but rather a gap between two other days. It's the silence from the flat next-door that makes you think that something must be wrong. It's the quiet small talk on the other side, still in bed and still not sure what to make of this in-between day. It's the usually so busy streets outside, usually filled with angry cars trying to be in time for once after 30 years at the same job. But now it's empty, clean and pure. I open my eyes, sneak downstairs and then the passed out guys on the couch. It smells like old vineyards filled with corps and the empty bottles are not standing up anymore. A sudden burst of sorry came over me and I couldn't help but feeling sad. It's sad because we do this thing. How someone decided that one day every week is a little better than all the other ones, so let's drink until we can't remember the other ones, and then we use the day after as a meaningless transportations-day to Monday. Then we can do it all over again.

I opened the door with a creek and couldn't care less if I woke the youth up. The youth, I should probably include myself in that genre. I'm the youngest one in this house after all. I took a deep breath and filled my soar lungs with purity and clean oxygen. Inhale reality, exhale sleep and tears. I made my way through the park and over the fields with slow unconcerned steps. After all it was Sunday, I had no destination, no time or place, no task but to make the best of what I'd been given.

On love.

Some days I wake up and it feels like I haven't slept at all, still exhausted from the endless running in my mind and I'm still unable to move one inch. But then some days I wake up and have to hold my own fists back to not break the nearest window, like today because I dreamt of you and that always leaves me angry. The world is filled with so many beautiful people after all and who am I to think that you will hold on, hold on to me, because who am I

and what are we?

I'm losing myself in this dream of us because you're just the most beautiful thing I've ever seen, but I can't seem to figure out my feelings towards this creation and where am I to go now?

I'm reading old poetry and asked Petrarch himself about the secret, the secret to his 366 sonnets about the love of his life. What did he do when she left him alone and how did he stand the unbearable lack of himself? Was it worth it? All these 366 poems about his beating heart, did they comfort him or trigger her memory? And is that what being an artist means, being a poet? To sacrifice yourself for your art, sacrifice your heart for your art, because it's only through something broken that something beautiful can grow, and is that the soul of these 366 sonnets?

Was it worth it?

I'm practicing Zen and reading Rumi and why does no one ever mention the fact that both Romeo and Juliet killed themselves? Their love equalled suicide, and so now tell me dear Mr. Alfred Tennyson, tell me I'm still supposed to believe that it's better to have loved and lost than to not have loved at all,

because I am in doubt.

Who am I to think I know anything about what these great poems means, but no matter what I read or learn it all goes back to the answer I don't want to have, because I was safe in my independence and now it's nowhere to be found and still –

who am I and what are we?

I had my life and death carefully planned out, a few searching years with no one close enough to distract me, and now –

who am I
and who are we
and will it mean anything in the end?

> "Tis better to have loved and lost
> Than never to have loved at all."
> – Alfred Tennyson

Duende. The possibility of loss.

I had you for a while, but now you're gone and I'm back to swallowing my own pride. We loved for a while, well you did, I never stopped even though I never did it very well.

Please know I'm doing okay . . .. well, at least I'm holding on the best I can and today I even got out of bed before it was time to go back again.

I'm still never really hungry, but it doesn't bother me very much and it doesn't even hurt anymore because my muscles are strangely numb, you see, I can break this glass in my bare hand and it doesn't even hurt, strange, you see? Broken glass and open wounds, now isn't that beautiful?

x xx I wear you on my skin

Some nights I make myself dinner and these chemicals have never burned my throat sweeter. I fall asleep with the sun still shining through my window, exhausted from the reliving of you and I, or the you and I my mind made up, because of these chemicals, sweetly burning my throat, and I know it's not very good for my voice but I haven't felt like singing lately any way.

Other nights I'm wandering endlessly along the river, trying to end up somewhere, where I'm not to be found.

See, I had you for a while, but now you're gone and I am trying to go on living, because what else is there to do? I'm back to relearning myself again, because everything I learned with you can't stay and so, let's get back to basic -

who am I and what are we?

Yeah, yeah, I'm reading Rumi and practicing Zen and Petrarch still hasn't answered me about these 366 sonnets, but I guess this is when I should start writing if I ever will have a chance to finish them.

... As a matter of fact, I've already written at least 366

sonnets about you and I'm sick and tired of seeing your face every time I sit down to write. I'm tired of feeling your hands on my skin every night I try to sleep and I no longer want to expect your name when I get a text.

Actually, I hate writing this and I still hate it even though I can't stop and I no longer want to think of you but I cannot get you out.of.my.head.

Self-destruction has never felt so sweet and this bottle has never been so empty. Give me a sharp edge, I have bones to break and skin to split and how deep must I cut to carve you out of my heart? How much skin must I peel to kill the echoes of your fingerprints that you left there to burn. Burn. Burn, you made me burn like a fucking fire with your energy and spirit and - bullshit. You were greedy and talked ugly and beautifully and wanted more, more, more and I couldn't

have loved you any . ..

more . ..   .. . and please know

I gave

my all.

It was a pleasure to burn.
Now my fire is gone and so it's time for me to go back to doing this thing on my own.

> *"I can write the saddest poem of all tonight:*
> *I loved her, and sometimes she loved me too."*
> - *Pablo Neruda*

Dec 13, 2012

I want to write about the things that matter, that makes your stomach turn inside out. My fingers run smoothly over the keys once they get started, like a ceremony of truth, no one's left in mercy.

I indulge myself in my heavenly destruction and this empty bottle makes such a beautiful reflection in this broken mirror, reflecting the insides of my inconsistent mind.

I follow my vein with the tip of my finger, the one that gets more defined every day, as if it's trying to break out and split my skin. From my hands, pressing hard over my wrist, up to my heart. It's still flowing in there, maybe, looks like a frozen river under this pale skin.

There are days when I have to lie completely still for ten minutes before I can feel my own pulse, and it's beating slower, fading fast.

It will get harder from here and I'm collecting my locks, writing my letters, isolating my walls. I never meant to make you concerned and please don't worry, but lover, it will get harder from here.

I am not your weekend morning with coffee and roses. I am insomnia and nausea and every night when you're off in sleep I'm staying up counting my bones, discussing my choices with the voices in my head.

I thought I could get rid of my old ways, my old habits, my old me this way, but I'm coming to the conclusion that one's own personality is independent from its body and so I can keep this up until there's nothing left but my skeleton, but my mind will still be in there, you see? And so now I need to study. I need to follow the signals from my brain to my heart and do you know any scientists because I am open for experiments. I am open for observations and you can study me like Woyzeck, use my very brain for analysis, because I swear I'm an exceptional case.

It will get harder from here and December was never gentle with me, but I'm ready for battle.

Don't worry lover, I've been sharpening my knives and I can sit in lotus for hours. I'm ready to face the monsters. You go your way and I will try to still be here, if you choose to come back.

There comes a time when you have to make the decision to either surrender and let the storm bury every trace of your very existence,

or to stand up and defend your own life.

If you say I have something to fight for, I will fight.

They all wanted me to shrink.

"Fit in here, you're the wrong shape, don't rise, small - small - small is the way - shrink."

And I think I confused the head with the body, the mind with the matter, because suddenly I took it all so literally. I made myself shrink and now it's just too hard to stop. The adrenaline is too addictive and my heart has never felt so alive, racing to the rhythm of the music I hear in my head every night. The pills are tasting sweeter every time and the chemicals don't even burn my throat anymore, leaves a craving for something stronger,

~~x   xx~~   setting me on fire .. .

I want to burn. Are there any feelings left?

And I find it pretty amusing how I never managed to convince anyone of my worthiness, my potential, but I seem to have convinced them all that they too meant the body over head, the matter of mind, because they talk nicer to me now. Talking slower, sweeter, calmer, as if I'm something to notice, something to be aware of.

You're aware of me now, aren't you?

Suddenly no harsh words about my art or my sorrow. Just calm beautiful phrases, nicely asking

"are you ok?"

How you think I don't notice the way you're looking at me now. I could feel your eyes on me from the other side of the ocean and you better take a good look at me now because soon enough you won't be able to take your eyes off me. You won't be able to find any sweet words anymore and soon enough there won't be anything left to look at

and so now I dare you to tell me that I am the wrong size, the wrong shape. Tell me again that I need to shrink, because I still confuse the head with the body, the mind with the matter, and I know exactly what I'm doing but I've lost control and that's what makes it interesting.

I'm running with the haunted, laughing with the devil

and don't touch me because you will burn. I set myself on fire because no one else did, and you won't see me surrender. Only walking away, slowly, never to look back. Wading in the ocean, walking at the bottom of the sea, because my insides are rotten and I'm ready for justice.

I'm ready for honesty and braveness and I will pay the price it took to be noticed. I will pay the price it took to not grow up but to shrink because that's what they all told me to do and now I'm ready for destruction and sharp edges.

"I thought I wanted to be a poet, but all I ever wanted was to be a poem."

Watch me shrink.

~~You won't be able to take your eyes off me.~~

I will love you like the world is ending.

One day I won't be here anymore.
One rainy day you won't find me laying beside you in
bed when you wake up.
One day there will be no kissing in the morning
or coffee and cigarettes while waiting for the day to start.
There will be no more holding hands or texts starting with
fire and ending with *love*.

One day I won't be here anymore,
so maybe you can care about us now?
Maybe you can shelter us and treat this as if it won't
    last
and as if each morning is the last morning,
and each kiss is the last kiss,
because I fear you're taking this for granted,
and I know there are so many other great things you've had,
and I know I might not be that special,
but you're by far the greatest thing I've ever had.

Soon enough I won't be kissing you awake,
Because I feel this is the beginning of my end, darling,
I'm hurting in quite a lot of ways,
and I never learned to stay
so I need to tell you, love,
that one day I won't be here anymore.
And maybe then you can miss me a little bit?
Because I will be missing you for the rest of my days,
I even miss you when I'm with you because I know that it
won't last,
    and it's quite a heavy burden,
    a heavy burden for my shrinking body to have.

So for now,
I will miss you like I'll never see you again,
And the next time I see you,
I will kiss you like I'll never kiss you again,
And when I fall asleep beside you
I will fall asleep as if I'll never wake up again,
because I don't know if I will.
I don't know if I will.

I will love you like the world is ending,
because I fear it is.
I will love you like my faith is calling,
because I fear it is.
I fear it is.
I fear it is.

Someone should have told me this.

It was beautiful and it was true and for the first time in my
life I felt alive.
    I was alive.
Because I knew and you knew and no words were needed
    because we both knew.
And how we laughed and talked and walked hand in hand
    wherever we could walk
        hand in hand
because it didn't matter if it was raining or sunny,
    night or day, because I was
        with you.
And I was happy, and safe
    and that was all it took for me
        to be happy.

But I was young
    and didn't know better
and someone should have told me to capture every second
    every kiss
        every night
Because now I'm sitting here alone and it's getting really
hard to breath from those tears growing in my throat and
they want to break out, but there are people
        watching
    and I just want to be somewhere silent
        somewhere still
But I don't want to be alone because I'm scared and
            lonely
    and I don't understand
Because I was alone my whole life
    My whole life
I was so god damn lonely and I was content with that

because I liked myself and my own company
and I didn't need anyone
  I thought
Until I found you
  and it all changed.

In one week
One night
A few explosions
Some fireworks
  a comet
And I was changed.

So now I can't be alone
because you stole my independence
my ability to live alone.
Because you showed me company and love
  and what it's like to belong.
So now I can't go back
  to that bottom
    that cold ground
and please don't leave me alone, because it's too quiet
  too still
and I need noise or loud music and ecstasy to kill these rocks
  in my throat
    'cause I can't breathe
    and I hurt.   *I hurt.*

... xx.. xx x

So someone should have told me
  that love is not a Sunday morning
  with coffee and safety and comfort in your arms
  because I
    am in pain.

And I do not know what to do because all I can think of is you and it's hard
  because I just do.not.know.what.to.do.

So
  Someone should have told me that love is for those few brave
    who can handle the unbearable emptiness,
    the unbearable guilt and lack of oneself,
  for I lost myself to someone I love
  and I might get myself back
  one day
    but it will take time.
  This will take some time.
    Maybe one day
    I will belong to myself again
  Until then, I am yours, I'm all yours to keep
  and I belong with you
    Belong to you in any way you want.

          But you don't want me anymore.

  I wish someone would have told me this.
    someone should have told me this.

March 21, 2013
It was too hard to love.
    I was too hard to love.

There will be a new day, every day.

The days flash by without my notice,
the way you lose track of when to be awake and asleep,
the way you lose track of when to eat and when to shower,
the way you disappear when you lose something you love,
   someone you love.

And I'm taking the same way home
but suddenly it feels a thousand miles longer
and my legs can't seem to carry the weight of myself
   and this heaviness
in myself, in my eyes, in my heart
makes me wanna lay down and just rest
for maybe a second, or two,
because it's tiring
   to be this sad
         and alone.

But I know there comes a time in every tragedy,
in every grief
in every one's life
when you wake up one morning and you don't feel as heavy.
There will come a day,
when you wake up after actually being able to sleep for once
   and you will notice the sun again.
The rain stopped and left the air clean and pure,
and you notice how the winter disappeared
         somewhere on the way
and it's spring again.
You will open the window, let the air into your hidden room,
and it will not be as a hard to breathe anymore,
not as hard to stand up,
not as hard to simply be.

There comes a time for healing
no matter how broken you are right now,

No matter how heavy your heart is right now.
There comes a time when you will be able to go outside
and let the sun shine on your face
and let the wind touch your hair
and you will not be tired by just simply be awake.
There comes a time when you will be happy to be alive again
and that day you will appreciate your own being
because now you know the other side.
Now you know the opposite.
Now you know what it's like to not be sure if you really are,
who you really are,
if you simply are,   anymore.
And that day
   will be the beginning of everything.

Until then I will watch the tulips bloom and die and be replaced,
because that's what they give you when you're sad,
because flowers are nice to look at,
   they say,
But I'd rather look at you,
and the way I'm recalling every movement,
every little thing you do,
When you're deep in thought about something,
When you're trying to figure out what I just said,
When you're drunk and lose your guard.
But you're not here anymore
so the tulips will have to do,
until I will wake up one day,
and notice how the rain stopped,
and then I will go outside and take a long walk by the ocean
and realize that there is still beauty in the world,
even without you.
   Beauty,
      even without you.

Until then, I will watch the tulips bloom and die and be replaced.
   I am still in pain.

Epilogue - *Amor Fati.*

March 30, 2013

This is the beginning of the rest and I'm digging up old diaries. Reviewing goals and finding old pictures of a girl I can't recognize anymore. I'm turning the picture back and forth, changing the angle, switching the light, observing every line. She remains a mystery.

I'm reading old lists and cluttered pages of things I wanted to achieve, what I wanted to be and where I wanted to go. It was just a few years ago I packed my life in a bag and left that sweet hell called my home and I had no intention to return. I wanted a new start, a new me, a new life.

I read and wrote and sang and learned and a year later I had my whole future mapped out, carefully written down and I was ready to give my whole existence to it. I wanted the world or nothing at all. I wanted to be thrown into the ocean and fight my way back, only to prove that I could survive. I wanted them to know that they didn't break me.

But then life happens and things don't really turn out the way you planned. You learn the hard way that more often than not your plans will be ruined and laughed at by people you didn't even invite into your life, and they won't care. You learn that the things you thought would be easy weren't that easy at all and the things you thought you'd never achieve turned out to be easy as a breath. I spent nights scared and alone in the middle of nowhere, with nothing but my guitar and a long lost dream, fading every day. I spent nights behind walls of comfort, safe in loving arms. I walked for hours on aching muscles, following whatever there was to follow, and I learned to build my home in whatever there was to build a home in.

I lost friends and gained friends. I left and came back and gave up and then stood up again. I've seen the sunset from a cliff by the ocean and I've seen the sunrise over a foreign city before the world was existing and awake. I lost track and my belief in if music was meant for me, only to come back with a new perspective on how beautiful it can be when you give up the struggle, the future and the expectations. When you dare to let go of the ugliness and the clouds and the darkness that you so easily embrace when things don't really go your way.

I've had so many letters sent to me this year, telling me stories about scars and heartbreak, starving and not being able to find a purpose. Sometimes it's just a need of telling someone, putting the struggle on paper so that it feels real, not just in your head. And I'm here, I will listen and I will care. I will never say no. But then sometimes I get these letters filled with question marks. Filled with open answers, waiting for me to finish.

Listen; I'm one of you. I'm seeking, I'm searching, I'm studying and I'm learning. Sure, there are days when I feel strong and determined and I know exactly what I want and where to go and nothing can stop me. But know that there are days when I'm back to breaking mirrors. Know that there are days when I can't eat, run for hours, hurt people I love and lie my way out of trouble. I'm one of you and just like you I'm writing letters to myself with question marks and unfinished lines, waiting for someone to find and finish.

This winter was hard and I wasn't sure if I'd make it through. I was cold and small and felt ugly and useless because what if I wouldn't be able to finish what I started? What if this great talk about albums and books and "become the best that you can be" was just empty words spoken by the young girl I used to be. What if these new people I'd met, the new life they taught me, the new passions I'd grown, meant that my strength was gone. What if through opening up and giving pieces of myself to someone else, meant that I also lost the part of me that I needed to be that determined person I used to be.

Look, I was alone and I was worried and scared and cried myself to sleep until I stumbled upon someone so beautiful that the world felt safe. I found someone who took my worries away, for a while, and it felt like home. I wanted to build a home there, because it felt sheltered. Peaceful. Calm. And I was tired. And sure I could have had a wonderfully quiet and uneventful life, safe behind his walls, but that's not what this is supposed to be about. Not what love is supposed to be about.

Months went by and I realized that I didn't belong to myself anymore. I belonged to expectations; from myself and from other people. I belonged to my past; to who I used to be and the girl people still thought I was. And most of all; I belonged to someone else, who I'd come to love. I couldn't find a way to both give my love to someone and still belong to myself, and I felt both free and imprisoned in the new comfort of having other people close and around. I just couldn't stand it. I couldn't figure it all out.

I started to shrink because I thought that that's what they all wanted me to do. And because I thought that if I just could become smaller, less visible, they wouldn't notice me and I could carefully disappear and withdraw from this place. I also knew that struggling with the delicate balance between love and freedom was nothing new. People have been writing about this since the beginning of time, and I figured there have to be something to learn. So I read. I read poetry and literature and drama and theatre. I practiced meditation, the teachings of Buddha, philosophy and mythologies. I studied politics and history and there is not one single self-development book on the market I haven't heard of. I lost myself in learning and somewhere in between the pages I found fragments of the art of living, of thoughts, that would slowly shape my own personal philosophy. My own philosophy and definition of a life lived well, and I learned to keep it treasured, hidden and sacred. Because I needed it to belong to me. It felt like I lost pieces of me in everything I did. Through opening up to my fans online, by releasing my music, letting my friends really get to know me, and I needed my world to belong to me again. That's the trouble with letting people know about your thoughts, your opinions and ideas. The moment you tell someone, they don't belong to you anymore. They're open for the world to take and tear apart, and I need to have my own world. My own place where I am the one who get to decide the value of things. The value of my life. The value of me. And that's the contrast. First they screamed that I was too hidden, too hard to get to know. Then they said I was changed and not myself. And then I was once again too secret, too private.

So look, I never said it was easy to find your place in this world, but I'm coming to the conclusion that if you seek to please others, you will forever be changing because you will never be yourself, only fragments of someone you could be. You need to belong to yourself, and let others belong to themselves too. You need to be free and detached from things and your surroundings. You need to build your home in your own simple existence, not in friends, lovers, your career or material belongings, because these are things you will lose one day. That's the natural order of this world. This is called the practice of detachment.

Change is hard, but it's the only thing you can be completely sure about. Things happen even if you're standing still, and until you learn the natural order of this universe you will never be free. Go outside that door for a second and you will not be the same person walking in again. I have it written on my walls; learn detachment and you shall be free; learn to dance with the sorrows of the world; you were never not coming here. *Amor Fati.*

The philosophers I now call my teachers and mentors are the great thinkers who wrote about this; the concept of loving your fate. Friedrich Nietzsche, Joseph Campbell and Seneca had it all figured out. The trusting of your story. Of how you were never not coming here. Of no matter how hard or ugly or painful your situation might be, you were meant to get there or here because it will teach you something you need to know in the future. Life will never throw you anything that you're not supposed to be able to handle, or learn to handle. How comforting is that, to know that everything you're going through is for your own advantage?

And so there was love and I know it's a wonderful idea that it's a destination, a safe harbor where you can arrive and stay and slowly perish, but that's not what you've been fighting for all these years. Not what this universe has in store for you.

The Buddhists have told me about detachment a thousand times over, the books I treasure as bibles and the philosophers I admire like Gods: Follow your bliss, go seek the Great Perhaps, run with the haunted and be forever searching, learning, exploring. For people like you, there are no destinations, only journeys. Only new beginnings, new adventures, and it's all a part of this great story you've been chosen for. It's already written for you, you just have to believe in the forces, the signs, telling you where to go and what to do. Trust the process. Stand up, damn it, and have some faith in yourself and your fate! Stop being so damn scared, you belong here! You have nothing to fear. You do know what to do and you do know where to go, just close your eyes and start to see. Stop wishing you were meant for smaller things!

Sorry for the preaching, all I mean is; you need to trust your story. You're not supposed to stay anywhere, even for a day, as the same person or in the same place or with the same people, even though it feels like a very comfortable idea.

So kid, listen; I know it hurts and I know there are days when you wake up in the middle of the night and can't breathe because of this unbearable lack of something, of someone. (Of him and of yourself, because you let yourself belong to someone else, and now it's time to take it back). But know that it was all just a part of the plan, your plan, your fate and it was meant to happen exactly as it did because look at you now! Look at the person the day before you met him or her, or the day before you left your home or the day before you embarked on that new adventure. Started that new job or applied for that college. And look at the person standing here now. You see what I mean? And there is nothing you will go through that is not within your story. It's already written, you see, and your only task is to live it and embrace it. To be the one who's turning it into action and to be the character you want to be remembered as. The hero you want to be remembered as. Now let me repeat and clarify this; the hero is not someone who set out on a journey without any setbacks. A hero is someone who will climb the mountain, survive storms, fall and stumble and get back up. To be the hero you need the trials, so embrace them.

Anyway, I know what it's like to be sad for no reason at all, or to literally have your heart ripped out, standing in the rain with no intention of surviving. I know what it's like to love someone so much that you can't imagine existing without that person, and what it feels like when he says that he just doesn't love you anymore. So I know it hurts, I hurt, and I'm not saying that it will go away anytime soon, or that it won't come back again. But what's so wrong with being a little lost? What's so wrong with being scared or worried or tired? I'm sure as hell wouldn't have written this book if it wasn't for the bony elbows, the ugly words, the lost friends or the sleepless nights. Remember all those nights you cried to the Gods and thought that "this is it". And remember how you suddenly realized something, learned something, slowly found a new path, and then woke up one morning and realized that you survived. You made it through. And oh how lucky you are that the other path didn't work, because obviously it wasn't meant for you!

Life can be so beautiful and wonderful things are waiting for you. I know it, I've had a taste of it, small moments of complete clarity. Magical nights under the stars and peaceful mornings with someone you love, and before you know it you will thank yourself for staying strong and holding on. I do, most of the days. And the other days I try to keep my eyes on the track and remember to enjoy my story. Of taking my sorrow in my own hands and create something from it. Like a song, a poem, or this; this book.

I know there are days when even one single positive thought feels like too much effort, but you must develop an unconditional love for life. You must never lose your childish curiosity for the possibilities in every single day; who you can be, what you can see, what you can feel and where it can lead you. Be in love with your life, everything about it. The sadness and the joys, the struggles and the lessons, your flaws and strengths, what you lose and what you gain. (Hey, remember I'm just like you, I'm still trying to practice this myself, I just think it's something worth striving for. And I'm just thinking that if I can find comfort in these thoughts, this philosophy, then maybe you can do too?)

So here's to growing, discovering and exploring. Here's to everything we will be, see, feel and do. Here's to music, art, poetry and all things beautiful. And here's to letting it touch us. Touch us so deep that it becomes a part of us. Don't just read poetry, don't just sing, don't just practice guitar or "work" as a lawyer - live it. Breathe it. Let it consume you, write it on your skin, and your very existence shall be a great story.

I want my life to be the greatest story.

My very existence will be the greatest poem.

Watch me burn.

Love always,
Charlotte

So there it is. The story of me. My first published book. A small little idea of making my story come alive became another dream that I went for, and I hope this can inspire someone else to go after their dream. You can do it, I swear, if you just want it bad enough.

Now that I've let you in under my skin and inside my mind, please come find me online and say hi, I want to get to know you. And if you liked my story, my journey, and want to help me tell the world about it, it would mean the whole world if you wanted to just write a few nice words about it as a review on Amazon & Goodreads.com. And please tell all your friends, family, classmates and enemies about it. I'm nothing without you and your help.

Thank you for being you.
Charlotte

www.CharlotteEriksson.com
www.twitter.com/justaGlassChild
www.facebook.com/TheGlassChild
www.theGlassChild.bigcartel.com
www.TheGlassChild.tumblr.com
www.Youtube.com/aGlassChild
TheGlassChildMusic@gmail.com

28960294R00070

Made in the USA
Middletown, DE
02 February 2016